Letter to an Influential Atheist

Roger Steer

Authentic
LIFESTYLE

First published in 2003 by Authentic Lifestyle

09 08 07 06 05 04 03   7 6 5 4 3 2 1

Authentic Lifestyle is an imprint of Authentic Media,
PO Box 300, Carlisle, Cumbria CA3 0QS, UK
and Box 1047, Waynesboro, GA 30830-2047, USA
www.paternoster-publishing.com

British Library Cataloguing in Publication Data
A catalogue record for this book is available from the British Library

ISBN 1-85078-478-7

Typeset by Textype, Cambridge
Cover design by David Lund
Printed in Great Britian by Cox and Wyman, Reading

Contents

1 Dear Professor Dawkins   1

Wallace agreed with Juliet   2

Your most famous sentence   3

Where we disagree   5

Areas of agreement   7

2 The Mystery Darwin and Wallace Set Out to Solve   10

God and *The Origin of Species*   12

God and *The Descent of Man*   12

Darwin's 'loss of faith'   15

The verdict of Darwin's contemporaries   17

3 Alfred Russel Wallace   18

'One of the greatest scientists'   20

Where Wallace differed from Darwin   20

The limits to the power of natural selection   21

Wallace and consciousness   23

Free will   24

Science 'proves a spiritual dimension'   25

Darwinism 'supports man's spiritual nature'   26

Wallace on the cell   27

The complexity of the cell   28

The purpose of the universe   28

Preparing the earth for life   29

Temperature   30

Adaptation not inconsistent with design   31

Useful materials   31

Carbon   32

Wallace on water   32

Wallace on Darwin   33

Wallace on the wonder of birds   34

Making life possible   35

Darwin's distress   36

Wallace's spiritualism   37

Wallace and religion   39

Your forerunner   41

Opposition to Haeckel   42

Assessment of Wallace   42

Human distinctiveness   44

4 Evolution Today   47

The significance of the double helix   48

Self-replication   50

'Survival machines'   51

Genetic determinism   52

Reductionism   52

5 What Evolution Explains 54

The nature of our world 54

What is chance? 55

Natural selection does not operate in a vacuum 59

The universe as an expression of God's will 60

Human identity: Who are you? 61

Our sense of purpose 62

Why are we here? 64

Apparent purposefulness of evolution 66

Life's improbability 67

How natural selection got started: the origin of life 68

The fun of making babies 70

6 The Mind's Complexity 71

Whence this awareness? 75

Newman on mind 75

Mind at home with abstract concepts 77

The conscience 78

7 Consciousness 80

The uniqueness of human consciousness 81

The debate 83

Brain, mind, self and consciousness 84

The building blocks of consciousness 85

Not comparable to computers or AI 86

Denial of Self 88

The paradox of the Self 90

The idea of divine experience   91

8 God and the Universe   93
Mysterious, but orderly   94
The Anthropic Principle   96
The Creator with a pin   98
Einstein on coherence   99
The mysterious usefulness of mathematics   99
Did the universe know we were coming?   100

9 God and Baseball Hats   102
Religion and education   103
Your objections to God   105
Religion 'peddling an untruth'   106
Morality   107
'Intrinsic value'; beauty   109
The Christian idea of God   112
The Genesis account of creation   113
The Christian idea of creation   117
What do we mean by 'nature'?   118
What does 'automatic' mean?   120
Analogy   121
Revelation   121
Logos and creation   124
Evidence for the resurrection   125
Paley and the role of natural theology   126
God speaks today   129

The nature of truth 130

10 The Mystery of Suffering 132
The nature of faith 136
A warning 138

Notes 140
Bibliography 148

Foreword

David was a seriously unlikely hero – a slip of a boy facing a Giant Philistine – yet he won.

In this 'Letter to an Influential Atheist' (Professor Richard Dawkins) Roger Steer is surely being the David of our times. Arriving from a thatched cottage amongst the rolling hills of Devon he wanders off to the intellectual stream, collects a few well-chosen pebbles and one-by-one slings them at the Giant (Dawkins). Though not slain with one pebble, he may well be mortally wounded.

At last someone has stood up to Dawkins and, using many of the 'Giants' own words, has shown the failures and flaws in his atheistic gospel. Someone who is prepared to suggest that Dawkins' 'grasp of history is shaky' and his 'attacks on religious faith are tendentious and muddled' is certainly brave enough to be labelled 'David'. Furthermore, with one well-aimed slingshot the writer of this 'letter' demolishes Dawkins' skilful but misleading linkage of Wallace (co-developer with Darwin of the theory of evolution) with the view that evolution has solved the mystery of life and made atheism intellectually respectable. Indeed he points out 'Wallace argued precisely the opposite. His view was that scientific observations led inevitably to belief in a higher being'. He further observes that while Darwin and Wallace set out to solve the mystery of biological diversity Dawkins 'makes an unjustified leap in claiming that they solved the mystery of our existence'. 'This leap', says Roger Steer 'gets Dawkins into trouble', for, as he gently reminds Dawkins, on an American television interview he had agreed that asking 'why we are here at all' was a silly question. At this point in the 'letter' Dawkins' head is all but severed as Steer forcefully asserts 'You cannot tell us at one moment that Darwin and Wallace solved the mystery of our existence and then go on to tell us that we must not ask the ultimate questions about the purpose of the Universe'. Steer rubs salt into the wound by pointing out that it is at such places as Oxford, where the Giant is based, that for centuries dons and students alike have dared to ask exactly that sort of 'silly' question.

In one of his more conciliatory passages Steer 'warms to Dawkins' honesty' particularly with respect to Dawkins' comment that 'life is a huge statistical improbability' and that 'Darwinism does not provide us with either a complete or satisfactory explanation of various phenomenon' and then reminds Dawkins that this 'honest' admission does 'not sit happily with your claim that Darwin and Wallace solved the mystery of our existence'.

Arguing forcefully, but politely, through one well-reasoned point after another Roger Steer has achieved, like David, the improbable – he has made an intellectually robust Christian attack against the Giant atheist. Amongst Steer's questions he asks if we are entirely driven by the mechanistic self-replication of our genes, why should we 'see the barren frozen wasteland of the Antarctic as awesomely beautiful? . . . surely such an inhospitable place which has little or no food for us, and in which we have virtually no chance of survival should be frightening' and 'beauty, awe and wonder do not sit happily with your (Dawkins') view that evolution by natural selection explains our existence'. Perhaps surprisingly he does not ask why some people choose to have no children, or is that a flaw whereby our wills, part of the automata programmed by our genes, override the program that drives us?

So a superb 'letter' has done its job – or will history tell us otherwise – will Dawkins rise from amongst the heap of pebbles that now surround him and roar his atheism once more preaching again, as Roger Steer points out, 'what you seem to want people to believe' – 'that if something can be explained in scientific terms then it can no longer be regarded as created by God' (but what dictates the speed of light or the charge of an electron?). This atheistic message from the lofty spires of Oxford has gone almost unchallenged for far too long – and many people – often scientifically ill-informed – hear and believe – because of who Dawkins is, like the Philistines they recognise a Giant when they see one. But should such a Giant not have the intellectual depth to understand the untold damage he may have done through his own chosen distortion of the 'truth'? He has clearly felt the need to wage war on Christians – at last a Christian 'David' has risen from the crowd and with a few intellectual pebbles has, if not quite cut the Giants head off, shown up many of the flaws in his armour and the dangers of his arrogance.

For all who have read any of Dawkins' books this is a must and for those Christians who have avoided Dawkins because he is too painful or simply dismissed his views as unacceptable here at last is a well-reasoned case to help you.

Professor J. Roy Sambles FRS, F Inst P
School of Physics
University of Exeter

Dear Professor Dawkins

In your book, *Climbing Mount Improbable*, you recall a charming incident – one of those delightful cameos which have helped to keep your writing in the bestselling lists for a quarter of a century.

You describe how, when your daughter, Juliet, was six, you were driving her through the countryside. When Juliet pointed to some flowers by the side of the road, you asked her what she thought they were for.

'Two things,' she replied. 'To make the world pretty, and to help the bees make honey for us.'

You admit to being touched by this reply but you felt obliged to tell your daughter that it was not true. You acknowledge that Juliet's answer was much the same as that which most adults throughout history would have given. But you say we must all learn to see things through non-human eyes.

The truth is, you tell us, that flowers are not there for our benefit. They are for spreading copies of instructions for making more flowers, just as elephants are for spreading copies of instructions for making more elephants. The instructions are written in the language of DNA.

Flowers are nothing more than tools for getting DNA into the next generation. The bees are drawn towards the flowers and carry the pollen from one flower to another. It so happens we have a world full of pretty flowers, but the fact we enjoy looking at them is beside the point.[1]

Wallace agreed with Juliet

You do not tell us whether you persuaded your daughter to change her mind. I hope, however, that you told her about the distinguished scientist who contemporaneously but independently of Darwin arrived at the theory of evolution by natural selection and who agreed with her and not with you.

Quite rightly, whenever you refer in your writing to Darwin's momentous insight, you link his name to that of Alfred Russel Wallace, about whom I shall have more to say later in this letter. There can be no doubt about Wallace's orthodoxy in his adherence to the mechanism of natural selection: indeed he described himself as 'more Darwinian than Darwin' in this respect. But it is over the power of natural selection as an *explanation of the mystery of our existence* that Wallace differed to some extent with Darwin and totally with you.

Wallace agreed with Darwin in linking the origin and development of flowers to the visits of insects. He thought that the advantage of some species of flowers being conspicuous and unlike others flowering at the same time avoided the frequent crossing of species. Like your perceptive daughter, however, he did not believe that this was a complete explanation for colour in nature.

Wallace noted that the blue of the sky, the tints of sunset, the snow-covered mountains and the many shades of green in the country are unending sources of pleasure. He maintained that there is a relationship between this wealth of colour and our emotional and moral natures. Everyone can admire and delight in the cheerful colours of flowers, birds and insects. Why should the gorse on the moor be clothed in gold? Surely colour is there for us to enjoy.

Think of the delicate colours of the butterfly or the humming-bird, the smallest and most brilliantly coloured bird in the world, which Wallace had seen in his travels in the Amazon basin. He knew well that Darwinism taught that colour has its uses in nature. But he did not rule out the common sense view taken by Juliet that these colours are there for our enjoyment.

For Wallace, colour reinforced his belief in some guiding power, some supreme mind, directing and organising the forces of nature. He simply could not believe that human enjoyment of colour had been developed only as a survival strategy in the struggle for existence. Our love of colour, along with our appreciation of scenery and music were, in his words, 'gratuitous gifts' and powerful arguments for 'a benevolent Author of the universe'.[2]

Both Wallace's thinking, and Juliet's instinctive response to your question, are in line with Genesis 2:9: 'And the Lord God made all kinds of tree grow out of the ground – trees that were pleasing to the eye and good for food.' In similar vein, the astronomer Johannes Kepler wrote: 'We do not ask for what useful purpose birds do sing, for song is their pleasure since they were created for singing.'[3]

Your most famous sentence

Your books have been extraordinarily influential even in the minds of thousands of people who've never read them. I decided to write this letter to you after reflecting on perhaps the most famous sentence you have ever written. You begin *The Blind Watchmaker* with these words: 'This book is written in the conviction that our own existence once presented the greatest of all mysteries, but that it is a mystery no longer because Darwin and Wallace solved it, though we shall continue to add footnotes to their solution for a while yet.'[4]

I am not a so-called 'creationist'. I happily accept that evolution by natural selection is a good description of the process that produces biological diversity. I am writing this letter because I think you claim too much for evolutionary mechanisms. You try to make them into a theory of 'life, the universe and everything', and a biological theory – even such a major insight as this – is not up to such a Herculean task. It is an abuse of science to take a good theory out of its scientific context and use it for ideological purposes.

The British science writer, John Gribbin, described *The Blind Watchmaker* as perhaps 'the most important evolution book since Darwin'[5] and its opening sentence is often praised. A.N. Wilson, in his book *God's Funeral*, says that the sentence 'deserves a prize'.[6] I think that this sentence in particular, and your influential books in general, distort your readers' thinking in at least six ways.

1. Despite the striking and assured tone of your famous sentence, you do not yourself actually believe that Darwin and Wallace 'solved the mystery of our existence' as from time to time you honestly admit.
2. You mislead people by suggesting that Darwin and Wallace set out to solve the mystery of our existence: the truth is that the puzzle they sought to unravel was more modest.
3. By repeatedly linking the two men's names in the way you do, you imply that they drew from the theory of natural selection the same philosophical conclusions as you do: in fact they did not agree in their estimates of the explanatory power of natural selection and neither man agreed with you.
4. You do not acknowledge how controversial the wider conclusions you draw from the theory of evolution by natural selection are among your own colleagues within the scientific community.

5. In vigorously proclaiming your view that the theory of evolution has made atheism intellectually respectable, you misrepresent the story of Darwin's alleged 'loss of faith' and totally ignore Wallace's insistence on the universe's essential spiritual dimension.
6. You either misunderstand or deliberately caricature the nature of Christian faith.

Where we disagree

Our disagreement, and it is a fundamental one, is over the *explanatory power* of the theory of evolution by natural selection; in other words we disagree about the philosophical and religious implications of Darwinism. I do not agree with you that what Darwin and Wallace discovered either solved the mystery of our existence or strengthened the case for atheism. I see natural selection as a description of the process that produces biological diversity; you want to convince the world that it is a more or less sufficient explanation for our existence in all its complexity.

In setting out the reasons why I disagree with you I shall not be seeking to make a 'knockdown' case for religious belief; in other words, I am accepting that if there were unanswerable arguments for either theism or atheism we should expect every informed and thoughtful person to be either a religious believer or an atheist, and clearly this is not the case. My objective is to draw attention to the weaknesses of your atheistic worldview. I think you have a problem in accounting for an orderly universe in which, over several billion years, mindless molecules have transformed themselves into mind, meaning, memory and morality; chemicals have produced complexity, creativity, consciousness and character; replicators have conveyed reason through countless generations so that we have a world of life, love, beauty, values, happiness, altruism, a sense of purpose (as well as pain and perplexity) and a widely held belief in God.

When I take issue with your assertion that Darwin and Wallace solved the mystery of our existence I want you to be clear what I am saying both about mystery and the nature of science. It is clear that you equate progress in our understanding of the universe with a resolution of its 'mystery' and that for you this process makes belief in God unnecessary. Hence atheism becomes 'intellectually respectable'.

My own position is that God is certainly a mystery in the sense that we can never fully know or understand him. But he is also a God who has spoken and revealed himself on the stage of human history especially in the life, death and resurrection of Jesus. Though God himself is ultimately incomprehensible, the remarkable thing about his universe is that there is much about it that seems to us to be understandable. It is our perception that the universe is comprehensible, which has made the pursuit of science possible.

Although the early chapters of Genesis are not written in the language of science, it remains true that without the dominance of the worldview of God as Creator it is unlikely that the scientific enterprise would have developed as rapidly and as effectively as it has; and Joseph Needham has suggested that one of the reasons that China failed to develop modern science was because it 'lacked the idea of (divine) creation'.[7]

At no point in my letter to you will I be using the word 'mystery' to describe phenomena that scientists do not understand; and I shall not therefore be claiming areas of current scientific ignorance as God's special preserve. If God is the Creator and sustainer of the universe, he is also the author of truth. Christians, scientists and the many Christians who are also scientists, have a passion for truth.

I have no doubt that science will continue to increase our understanding of many of the awesome marvels of our world, whether we are talking of the origin of life, genetic sequencing, or the working of the human brain and its relationship to consciousness. As science does so, our sense of wonder will be enhanced (not diminished) as it was for pioneers of modern science in seventeenth-century Europe.

Before I enlarge on these points, I want to say a word about the common ground I believe there is between us.

Areas of agreement

First, I agree with you when you suggest (as you did for example in your Dimbleby Lecture in 1996)[8] that it is worthwhile at least to strive towards something called *objective truth*. In your books, you certainly reveal and communicate the passion for truth which you claim for yourself. I say this, even though I think your grasp of history is shaky and that your attacks on religious faith are tendentious and muddled. That said, you do seem to be impressed by and indeed to care about the beauty, elegance and simplicity of the fundamental laws of nature. You appear to care about goodness, especially in the sense of the virtue of intellectual honesty and facing up to unpalatable facts.

I would judge that both of us have little in common with those so-called relativists who see no reason to prefer scientific views over whatever beliefs any person or group of people may happen to feel comfortable with irrespective of any objective truth criteria. I guess this puts the two of us in the same camp in opposition to postmodernists who, I take it, would be as sceptical of your grand narrative (evolution by natural selection as a sufficient explanation of the mystery of our existence) as they would be of mine (the Christian story of a Creator and sustainer of the universe). I assume we agree that if postmodernism were true then both the practice of religion and the pursuit of science would be futile. Roger Scruton was surely right when he said: 'The man who tells you truth does not exist is asking you not to believe him. So don't.'

Second, I agree with you that the amount of *apparently complex design* we see around us cries out for an explanation – although you should not assume that my observation that the world has features that suggest a designer is my primary reason for believing in God.

Third, I share your *sense of wonder* (in one interview you described it as 'poetic wonder') at the huge size and complexity of the universe and I certainly do not believe that religious people have a monopoly on this awe-inspiring appreciation of what we see around us. I admire the eloquence and enthusiasm with which you try to convey this sense of wonder to your audience.

Fourth, I am happy to accept that the theory of *natural selection makes sense of a wide range of data* derived from many disciplines – anatomy, physiology, biology, botany, zoology, mathematics, geology, geography, palaeontology, anthropology and so on. I know that all biologists, including many Christians, work successfully within the framework of evolutionary theory since it unites the various aspects of biology to make a coherent and satisfying story.

Darwin and Wallace discovered that the diversity of the living world may be described in terms of a theory of variation and a theory of selection. In the twentieth century, biologists were able to express the theory in more sophisticated terms by telling us that *variation* is caused by genetic mutations that occasionally affect the survival and reproductive fitness of individuals. *Natural selection* is the process whereby genes that promote the greatest reproductive success of individuals in a given environment are more likely to be passed on to the next generation. Evolution is the process that results in heritable changes in a population spread over many generations: genes mutate; individuals are selected; populations evolve.

2

The Mystery Darwin and Wallace Set Out to Solve

Prior to their discovery of natural selection, both Darwin and Wallace certainly saw themselves as setting out to solve a mystery. But it was nothing so grand as your 'mystery of our existence' – it was the more modest 'origin of species'. I think we can agree that a species is a group (a 'population') of organisms that interbreed with each other but not with other organisms.

Why is there a variety of life on earth with very many different species? In the early nineteenth century, most people who reflected on these things thought of species as in some way especially and separately created by God. One of the first to use the word 'mystery' when speaking of the origin of species was Darwin who called it 'the mystery of mysteries'. Wallace spoke in similar terms. Before leaving for his expedition to the Amazon, Wallace visited the Insect Room of the British Museum of Natural History and wrote in a letter to his friend Henry Bates of his dissatisfaction with 'mere local' collections: 'I should like to take some one family and study it thoroughly, principally with a view to the theory of the origin of species. I fully believe that a full and careful study of the facts of nature will ultimately lead to a solution to the mystery.'[9]

Wallace wrote later that while he was in the Malay Archipelago, 'the question of *how* changes of species could have been brought about was rarely out of my mind'.[10]

The idea of evolution in its more general sense of some kind of ordered linkage between living things was not new. Naturalists like Ray, Linnaeus and Buffon had been toying with the idea for well over a century. Linnaeus, the great classifier of species, had spoken of the need to 'pursue the great chain of nature till we arrive at its origin'[11] and had hinted at the possibility that perhaps not all species then alive had been created at the beginning. Buffon produced a definition of a species that was closer to the modern one and allowed for the possibility of change. He knew there were varieties within species but he did not know of any mechanism by which varieties could become new species. The 'mystery of mysteries' was the mechanism for evolutionary change and adequate evidence.[12]

The solution to this mystery would be one of the major scientific advances in history: but neither of the two men who cracked it saw themselves as 'solving the mystery of our existence'. They did not, for example, think that they had solved the problem of the origin of life. Two years after the publication of *The Origin*, Wallace resumed his friendship with fellow-naturalist Henry Bates and recorded that 'our thoughts were full of the great unsolved problem of the origin of life'.[13] The problem remains a mystery to this day – though no doubt our scientific understanding will improve.

And, throughout his life too, Darwin had little time for social Darwinists. He preferred to see evolution as a biological theory rather than as an explanation of everything.

God and *The Origin of Species*

Your books have been rather successful in proclaiming the message that Darwinism equals atheism. Actually the author of *The Origin of Species* was always as reticent about pronouncing on ultimate questions about the existence of God as he was about the origins of life. Even in late editions of his book, Darwin said that he could 'see no good reason why the views given in this volume should shock the religious feelings of anyone'.[14]

Charles Kingsley, the novelist and clergyman who went on to become Professor of Modern History at Cambridge, was delighted with *The Origin* and told Darwin that the theory of natural selection provided 'just as noble a conception of Deity, to believe that he created primal forms capable of self-development . . . as to believe that He required a fresh act of intervention to supply the *lacunas* which He Himself had made'. Darwin gladly reproduced Kingsley's words in successive editions of his book.[15]

God and *The Descent of Man*

In the 1860s Darwin worked hard on his book *The Descent of Man* (eventually published in 1871). His wife Emma, all her life a devout (Unitarian) Christian, read an early draft with misgivings and wrote in a note to her daughter: 'I think it will be very interesting but that I shall dislike it very much as again putting God further off.'[16] The gruelling work of writing the book brought Charles close to a state of nervous collapse.

Concerned about this, Emma wrote him a letter raising an issue about which she found it easier to write than speak:

I am sure you know I love you well enough to believe that I mind you suffering nearly as much as I should my own and I find the only relief to my own mind is to take it as from God's hand, and to try to believe that all suffering and illness is meant to help us to exalt our minds and to look forward with hope to a future state. When I see your patience, deep compassion for others, self command and above all gratitude for the smallest thing done to help you I cannot help longing that these precious feelings should be offered to Heaven for the sake of your daily happiness. But I find it difficult enough in my own case. I often think of the words, 'Thou shalt keep him in perfect peace whose mind is stayed on thee.' It is feeling and not reasoning that drives one to prayer.[17]

Moved to receive this letter, Charles wrote at the bottom 'God bless you.' When the book was eventually published, Emma was no doubt relieved to read the following paragraph:

I am aware that the conclusions arrived at in this work will be denounced by some as highly irreligious; but he who denounces them is bound to show why it is more irreligious to explain the origin of man as a distinct species by descent from some lower form, through the laws of variation and natural selection, than to explain the birth of the individual through the laws of ordinary reproduction. The birth both of the species and the individual are equally part of that grand sequence of events, which our minds refuse to accept as the result of blind chance. The understanding revolts at such a conclusion, whether or not we are able to believe that every slight variation in structure, the union of each pair in marriage, the dissemination of each seed, and other such events, have all been ordained for some special purpose.[18]

He makes a good point. When I was present at a north London hospital for the birth of my two sons, I remember thinking, *What a marvellous miracle – thank God for the gift of life!* I do not think this is an uncommon reaction and indeed I have never heard anyone exclaim, 'This "natural process" of childbirth which I'm witnessing removes the need for God!' Darwin explained the origin of man through the laws of variation and natural selection and considered that this had no more religious significance (for or against) than the birth of a baby. This is hardly the philosophy of a man who, according to you, has made it easier to be an atheist.

In his old age, people wrote to Darwin asking whether he believed in God. He replied once that a man could undoubtedly be 'an ardent Theist and an evolutionist'.[19] For himself, he had 'never been an atheist in the sense of denying the existence of God,'[20] but he still felt profoundly uncertain. If he had to wear a label, perhaps the word coined by Thomas Huxley suited him best: 'I think that generally (and more and more as I grow older), but not always, that an agnostic would be the most correct description of my state of mind.'[21]

You pour scorn on Pope John Paul II's 'Message on Evolution to the Pontifical Academy of Sciences', which takes the line that evolution is not contrary to Christian belief. The Pope's message states (just as Wallace did) that man is a unique spiritual being although it notes that the moment in evolutionary history when the transition to the spiritual occurred cannot be determined by scientific observation. You characterize this idea as the belief that 'there came a moment in the evolution of hominids when God intervened and injected a human soul into a previously animal lineage'.[22]

It is odd that you ridicule this idea since Darwin clearly believed it when he wrote, in *The Descent of Man*: 'Few persons feel any anxiety from the impossibility of determining at what precise moment in the development of the individual, from the first trace of a minute germinal vesicle, man becomes an immortal being; and there is no greater cause for anxiety because the period cannot possibly be determined in the gradually ascending organic scale.'[23] In a footnote Darwin refers his readers to a discussion of the subject by the Rev J.A. Picton – and the issue under discussion is at what point in the evolutionary story man became an 'immortal being', not whether or not he has a spiritual dimension.[24]

Darwin's 'loss of faith'

Andrew Marr, in a characteristically engaging programme about Darwin in the BBC's *Great Britons* series, accepted uncritically the line produced for him by his researchers that writing *The Origin* led Darwin to lose his faith.

In your book *River Out of Eden*, you quote Darwin: 'I cannot persuade myself that a beneficent and omnipotent God would have designedly created the ichneumonidae [parasitic wasps] with the express intention of their feeding within the living bodies of caterpillars'.[25] You speak of Darwin's 'gradual loss of faith', but to be fair you should have gone on to complete the quotation about the ichneumonidae. It is from a letter he wrote to the American Professor of Natural History at Harvard, Asa Gray, a devout and orthodox Christian. Darwin went on to write: 'On the other hand, I cannot anyhow be contented to view this wonderful universe, and especially the nature of man, and to conclude that everything is the result of brute force. I am inclined to look at everything as resulting from designed laws, with the details, whether good or bad, left to the working out of what we may call chance . . . But the more I think, the more bewildered I become; as indeed I have probably shown by this letter.'[26]

In his *Autobiography*, Darwin discussed his religious beliefs and pointed out that religion is not necessarily true because people say it is. However, he commented that:

> Another source of conviction in the existence of God, connected with the reason and not with feelings, impresses me as having much more weight. This follows from the extreme difficulty or rather impossibility of conceiving this immense and wonderful universe, including man with his capacity of looking backwards and far into the future, as the result of blind chance or necessity. When thus reflecting I feel compelled to look to a First Cause having an intelligent mind in some degree analogous to that of man, and I deserve to be called a Theist.[27]

He wrote a marginal note explaining that 'This conclusion was strong in my mind about the time ... when I wrote the *Origin of Species*, and it is since that time that it has very gradually, and with many fluctuations, become weaker. But then arises the doubt – can the mind of man, which has, I fully believe, been developed from a mind as low as that possessed by the lowest animals, be trusted when it draws such grand conclusions?'[28] Thus grew – not atheism – but a state of mind that he thought could best perhaps be described as a wavering agnosticism.

In their excellent biography of Darwin (described by Stephen Jay Gould in *Nature* as 'unquestionably the finest biography ever written about Darwin'), Adrian Desmond and James Moore have confirmed that Darwin became a supporter and donor to the South American Missionary Society (SAMS) during the last 15 years of his life.[29] He had become an admirer of Christian missionary work during his voyage on the *Beagle*, having first encountered the Yaghan Indians of Tierra del Fuego in 1832 and being struck by their 'savage and wild' appearance and uncivilized ways. Years later in correspondence with his lifelong friend, Rear Admiral Sir James Sullivan, a member of the SAMS committee, Darwin wrote of his great surprise at the changes taking place among the Tierra del Fuego Indians as a result of missionary efforts to evangelize and educate them. Sullivan kept Darwin regularly updated with news of missionary activities and his committee elected Darwin an honorary member of the missionary society. Darwin sent his final annual subscription to SAMS a few weeks before he died with a cover note that commented, 'Judging from the Missionary Journal the Mission on Tierra del Fuego seems going on quite wonderfully well'[30] – hardly the words of a man whose faith in God had been dramatically shattered, or who had opened for the world a path to atheism.

The verdict of Darwin's contemporaries

Following Darwin's death at the age of seventy-three in April 1882, he was buried in Westminster Abbey and given full national recognition by church as well as state. Most pulpits and every newspaper reassured the public that his theories were compatible with orthodox religious faith. The historian, Owen Chadwick, says that by 1885 most educated Christians had accepted that evolution and Christian belief were compatible, although there were some who continued to believe in a special act of creation for humans even while they accepted a theory of natural selection for the evolution of plants and animals.[31]

3

Alfred Russel Wallace

I began this letter by referring to the co-discoverer, with Darwin, of the theory of evolution by natural selection. Although you often link the two men's names, you omit to tell us an important fact of history. This is that while Wallace and Darwin respected each other – and Wallace was one of the pallbearers at Darwin's funeral – the two men never agreed about the explanatory power of natural selection.

Wallace was born in Gwent in 1823 and died ninety years later in 1913. He grew up in Hertford, worked as a surveyor and teacher in Leicester before travelling and then working as a naturalist first in the Amazon basin and later in the Indonesian Archipelago – where the 'Wallace Line' between Borneo and the Moluccas islands was named after him. Even in his twenties, as an eager young naturalist, Wallace adopted the view that the simplest facts of everyday life have an inner meaning and depend on the same general laws as those at work in what he called 'the grandest phenomena of nature'. He wrote: 'Everywhere, not here and there, but everywhere, and in the smallest operations of nature to which human observation has penetrated, there is purpose and continual guidance and control.'[32] Incidentally he never believed in *occasional* interventions in the course of nature by some outside force.

In 1856 he wrote a paper that embraced the idea of a 'general design' behind nature. Like Darwin, he read Malthus' *Essay on Population* and called it 'perhaps the most important book I read'.[33] Malthus refuted utopian ideas of the perfection of a human society arguing that such perfection carried with it the seeds of its own destruction by stimulating population growth so that 'the earth would at last be overstocked, and become unable to support its numerous inhabitants'.[34]

Later in his life Wallace described how he had hit on the idea of the survival of the fittest and, in two nights, penned the complete theory in twelve pages: 'On the Tendency of Varieties to Depart indefinitely from the Original Type'.[35]

He sent a memoir to Darwin from the Moluccas in 1858. Darwin was stunned to read Wallace's conclusion that 'there is a general principle in nature which will cause many varieties to survive the parent species, and to give rise to successive variations, departing further and further from the original type'.[36] It was a theory that Darwin had been struggling for twenty years to express in a publishable and defensible form.

Wallace's paper formed an important part of a submission to the Linnaean Society which first put into the public domain the theory of evolution by natural selection. Wallace's work modified and hastened the publication of Darwin's *Origin*. Darwin was at this time forty-nine and Wallace thirty-five. Twelve years later in 1870, Darwin wrote to Wallace: 'I hope it is a satisfaction to you to reflect – and a very few things in my life have been more satisfactory to me – that we have never felt any jealousy towards each other, though in one sense rivals.'[37]

Darwin told Henry Bates that, 'what strikes me most about Mr Wallace is the absence of jealousy towards me: he must have a really good, honest and noble disposition. A far higher merit than mere intellect.' Both Wallace's recent biographers (Shermer and Raby) have fallen in love with their subject, who spent his long life replying courteously and helpfully to his many admiring correspondents and encouraging eager young naturalists.

'One of the greatest scientists'

Although he never went to university, Wallace received honorary doctorates from the Universities of Oxford and Dublin, was made a professional member of all Britain's major societies, including the Royal Society, which also awarded him its Royal Medal and Darwinian Medal for his 'independent origination of the origin of species by natural selection'.[38] Serious press accounts referred to him as, for example, 'England's greatest living naturalist'[39] (1886) and at his death as 'one of the greatest scientists ever to live'[40] and 'the Grand Old Man of Science'.[41] Apart from his books, he wrote 508 scientific papers, of which 191 were published in the journal *Nature*.

Where Wallace differed from Darwin

Although their two names will always be coupled, you are disingenuous to ignore the fundamental differences between Darwin and Wallace, which largely revolve around the explanatory power of natural selection. It is probable that Wallace's name will remain second to Darwin's, not only because Darwin was the author of the magisterial *Origin of Species* but also because Darwin created a research programme which continues to this day. However, even a narrow version of Darwin's theory as it applied to nonhuman animals differed from Wallace's.

In reviewing below the differences between Wallace and Darwin, I do not wish to imply that in every case I agree with Wallace. I am pointing out that he raised some important broader issues, which in many ways he tackled in an intellectually more penetrating way than Darwin, and which lend no support to the wide-ranging conclusions which you draw from the theory of natural selection.

Eight years before his death, Wallace listed, with his usual clarity, the matters on which he differed from Darwin. He pointed out that whereas Darwin believed there was no difference between humanity's nature and animal nature, he, Wallace, believed that a different agency, similar to that which first produced organic life and then consciousness, came into play to develop the intellectual and spiritual nature of humanity.

On the issue of whether evolution has a direction, and if so who directs the process, you are wrong to imply that Wallace was on your atheistic side. It is true that Wallace was 'more Darwinian than Darwin' in his zeal to apply natural selection and find the adaptive significance of every structure and function of an organism. But he fervently believed that evolution must have been guided at all stages by some form of supernatural direction. He also believed that the same supernatural director prepared the earth for us to enjoy. This was for him the whole purpose of evolution.[42]

The limits to the power of natural selection

Wallace was well aware that people who were following the debate about evolution would be surprised to discover that he did not believe that all nature could be explained according to the principle of natural selection. But he insisted that there were limits to the power of natural selection. In 1870 he wrote that:

Just as surely as we can trace the action of natural laws in the development of organic forms, and can clearly conceive that fuller knowledge would enable us to follow step by step the whole process of that development, so surely can we trace the action of some unknown higher law, beyond and independent of all those laws of which we have any knowledge . . . It therefore implies that the great laws which govern the material universe were insufficient for this production, unless we consider . . . that the controlling action of such higher intelligences is a necessary part of those laws.[43]

According to Wallace, there are three stages in the evolutionary story that cannot be accounted for by natural selection:

1. The change from inorganic to organic, when the earliest vegetable cell, or the living protoplasm out of which it arose, first appeared.
2. The introduction of consciousness.
3. The existence in man of a number of his most characteristic and noblest faculties.

Wallace reflected on human features such as skin, hands, feet, the voice box and speech, the ability to sing, artistic notions of form, colour and composition, the ability to reason mathematically, the development of moral and ethical systems, the understanding of profound concepts of time, eternity and infinity.

How were all or any of these faculties first developed, when they could have been of no possible use to man in his early stages of barbarism? How could natural selection, or survival of the fittest in the struggle for existence, at all favour the development of mental powers so entirely removed from the material necessities of savage men, and which even now, with our comparatively high civilisation, are, in their farthest developments, in advance of the age, and appear to have relation rather to the future of the race than to its actual status?[44]

Why, in other words, have we developed brains so much bigger than we actually need for survival? His answer: there must be an overruling intelligence that wants to give humanity a special place in the universe. Wallace believed in a 'creative power' and a 'directive mind' and criticized those who spoke of the growth of living things as so simple and natural a process as to require no further explanation.

Wallace had no doubt that mind was predestined. He distinguished, as does Susan Greenfield, between 'mind' and 'brain' and believed that mind is the cause, not the consequence, of brain development. In other words, there is a cause of life independent of the organism in which it exists. He spoke of the 'life-giver' and the 'mind-giver'.[45]

Wallace and consciousness

I devote Chapter 6 of this letter to consciousness and your own honest admission of difficulties with this issue. Here I want to note that as early as the 1860s scientists struggled with the problem of the connection between the physical processes in the brain and consciousness – the self-awareness that is a feature of the activity of our minds. Wallace was well aware of Thomas Huxley's answer to the problem – that our 'thoughts are the expression of molecular changes in that matter of life which is the source of our other vital phenomena'.[46] This did not convince Wallace, who insisted that he was unable 'to find any clue in Professor Huxley's writings'[47] that came near to bridging the gap from molecules to thought. He believed that even if molecules were structured into levels of 'greater and greater complexity, even if carried to an infinite extent,' this 'cannot, of itself, have the slightest tendency to originate consciousness'.[48]

Consciousness, says Wallace, is qualitative not quantitative. It cannot be produced by piling on more molecules as if there were some critical mass which, once reached, produces consciousness.

> If a material element, or a combination of a thousand material elements in a molecule, are alike unconscious, it is impossible for us to believe that the mere addition of one, two, or a thousand other material elements to form a more complex molecule, could in any way tend to produce a self-conscious existence. There is no escape from this dilemma – either all matter is conscious, or consciousness is, or pertains to, something distinct from matter, and in the latter case its presence in material forms is a proof of the existence of conscious beings, outside of, and independent of, what we term matter.[49]

Consciousness either exists or it does not exist. 'We cannot conceive a gradual transition from absolute unconsciousness to consciousness because the mere rudiment of sensation or self-consciousness is infinitely removed from absolutely . . . unconscious matter.'[50]

Free will

Our own free will, claimed Wallace, cannot be explained by any known natural force; he referred to gravity, cohesion, repulsion, heat, electricity and so on. Therefore there must be another force which accounts for our free will. Without a supernatural force 'a certain amount of freedom in willing is annihilated, and it is inconceivable how or why there should have arisen any consciousness or any apparent will, in such purely automatic organisms'.[51]

His conclusion was dramatic and poetic:

If, therefore, we have traced one force, however minute, to an origin in our own will, while we have no knowledge of any other primary cause of force, it does not seem an improbable conclusion that all force will be will-force; and thus, that the whole universe is not merely dependent on, but actually is, the will of higher intelligences or of one Supreme Intelligence. It has often been said that the true poet is a seer and in the noble verse of an American poet we find expressed what may prove to be the highest fact of science, the noblest truth of philosophy:

God of the Granite and the Rose!
Soul of the Sparrow and the Bee!
The mighty tide of Being flows
Through countless channels, Lord, from Thee.
It leaps to life in grass and flowers,
Through every grade of being runs,
While from Creation's radiant towers
Its glory flames in Stars and Suns.[52]

I say more about free will later in this letter.

Science 'proves a spiritual dimension'

When Wallace argued that there were limits to the power of natural selection that could only be made good by a higher intelligence he was not falling into the god-of-the-gaps trap (which inserts God into gaps in our scientific knowledge thus running the risk that as scientific knowledge expands into new areas God is reduced in size and is in danger of disappearing altogether). Wallace's approach clearly escapes this danger and was far more robust. He believed that the philosophical and religious conclusions he drew from his observations of nature could be fully incorporated within the type of empirical science he had practised all his life.

He linked his argument to the familiar idea that we cannot prove the existence of matter, only its force – 'when we touch matter we only really experience sensations of resistance, implying repulsive force'[53] – and continued:

> These speculations [of a higher intelligence guiding the evolution of the universe] are usually held to be far beyond the bounds of science; but they appear to me to be more legitimate deductions from the facts of science . . . Philosophy had long demonstrated our incapacity to prove the existence of matter, as usually conceived; while it admitted the demonstration to each of us of our own self-conscious, spiritual existence. Science has now worked its way up to the same result, and this agreement between them should give us some confidence in their combined teaching. The view we have now arrived at seems to me more grand and sublime, as well as far simpler, than any other. It exhibits the universe as a universe of intelligence and willpower; and by enabling us to rid ourselves of the impossibility of thinking of mind but as connected with our old notions of matter, opens up infinite possibilities of existence, connected with infinitely varied manifestations of force, totally distinct from, yet as real as, what we term matter.[54]

Darwinism 'supports man's spiritual nature'

You regularly assert that Darwin and Wallace solved the mystery of our existence and have made atheism intellectually respectable. From a straightforward historical perspective you are plainly wrong to couple the two men together in the way you do. Wallace wrote in 1889:

The Darwinian theory not only does not oppose, but lends decided support to, a belief in the spiritual nature of man. It shows us how man's body may have been developed from that of a lower animal form under the law of natural selection; but it also teaches us that we possess intellectual and moral faculties which could not have been so developed, but must have had another origin; and for this origin we can only find an adequate cause in the unseen universe of Spirit.[55]

Wallace on the cell

Wallace took a special interest in the cell. He thought that all organic life forms begin with a cell and he stressed that a cell is not just a particle of protoplasm but an organized structure. His question was, 'organized by what?'

In Wallace's day, the biologist Thomas Huxley – the two men were friends – used to maintain that life itself was the organizing power.[56] Some botanists used the termed 'vital force'. The German naturalist, Ernst Haeckel (though an atheist), used to talk about a 'cell-soul'.[57]

Wallace insisted that none of these suggestions went to the heart of the problem. None of these people had suggested anything more than some 'force' – but force is a cause of motion, not a cause of organization. There must be something more than merely a force. There must be some agency that guides and coordinates the process which builds up that infinitely complex machine, the living organism. Wallace thought of the cell as being not only self-repairing, but also self-renewing, self-multiplying, self-adapting to its ever-changing environment, so as to be, potentially, everlasting.

To do all this, he believed that neither 'life force' nor 'vital force' nor the 'cell-soul' were adequate explanations. What was needed, he said, was 'a mind far higher, greater, more powerful than any of the fragmentary minds we see around us – a mind not only adequate to direct and regulate all the forces at work in living organisms, but which is itself the source of all those forces and energies as well as of the more fundamental forces of the whole material universe'.[58]

The complexity of the cell

As cell biology textbooks reminds us, the living cell is packed with tiny mechanical structures: minuscule tweezers, scissors, pumps, motors, levers, valves, pipes, chains and even vehicles. But of course the cell is more than just a bag of gadgets. The various components fit together to form a smoothly functioning whole, like an elaborate factory production line. Wallace correctly identified that the miracle of life is that the tiny parts of an organism are integrated in a highly organized way.

We may wonder how 'nature' discovered how to build the complex machine we call the living cell? Somehow, collectively, unthinking atoms get together and – as Paul Davies puts it so delightfully – 'perform the dance of life' with exquisite precision.[59] I have no doubt that biologists will discover more about how the various chemical components have been utilized to put together a living cell; and that Christians will see this as one of the more remarkable aspects of God's created order as described by science.

The purpose of the universe

You deny that the universe has any overall meaning or purpose. It is just there. In his book, *Darwinism, An Exposition of the Theory of Natural Selection with Some of its Applications*, Wallace wrote: 'To us, the whole purpose, the only *raison d'être* of the world – with all its complexities of physical structure, with its grand geological progress, the slow evolution of the vegetable and animal kingdoms, and the ultimate appearance of man – was the development of the human spirit in association with the human body.'[60]

Wallace believed that the universe has a purpose: it exists for the development of human beings. This view is not fashionable today and you have no time for it. But the co-discoverer of the theory of natural selection believed that humans are the crowning product of the whole cosmic process of life-development. Humans are the only living things who can begin to understand nature and trace its ways of working. We alone can appreciate hidden forces at work around us.

Beyond all the phenomena of nature, says Wallace, there is mind and purpose. And the ultimate purpose is the development of humankind for an enduring spiritual existence. He thought of the universe as slowly progressing towards a predestined end. He believed that humans should take responsibility to look after their heritage from the past on behalf of future generations.

Preparing the earth for life

Wallace described the mechanical, physical and chemical adjustments of the earth's surface that he thought were essential to the development of life. He did not believe that any other planet had the conditions right for the development of life. He believed that the overriding mind so ordered the forces at work in the universe as to make possible the improbable sequence of events that led to life on earth.

Wallace thought we should think not only of mind-action, but of *guidance*. In other words, in addition to the processes that are involved in natural selection and adaptation through survival of the fittest, there is a far higher mind that foresees all possible results in the growth of our cosmos.

He spoke of the forces that have been at work in continually remoulding the earth's surface. He argued that the frequent changes in the environment produced by these forces have been the initial causes of the corresponding changes in the forms of life, owing to the need for living things to adapt to the changed conditions. The changes in the earth's surface have opened up new places in nature to be successively filled through evolution as an end result of variation and the struggle for existence.[61]

Temperature

Wallace invited people to consider the temperature of the human body. Somehow the human body makes the complex, precise and difficult changes needed to keep all the circulating fluids and internal organs at a constant temperature, varying only by a few degrees Celsius.

Think, said Wallace, of those cosmic adjustments, which, during many millions of years, have preserved the earth's surface within the limited range of temperature that allows for the development of life. That the temperature of the earth should have been kept within such narrow limits as has been achieved since the Cambrian period of geology – when the first primitive forms of life appeared – is remarkable when we remember that the world has always been losing heat by radiation. As the earth loses heat by volcanoes and hot springs, these losses are counteracted by heat from the sun and the conservation effect of our moisture-laden atmosphere. The maintenance of constant temperature requires, says Wallace, some guiding power over cosmic forces.[62]

Adaptation not inconsistent with design

There was a consistency in Wallace's position – in the balance he achieved between his passionate belief in evolution by natural selection and his conviction that evolution requires direction. He knew that animal life depends on plant life. According to the theory he had developed, he recognized that the entire organization of animal life would, by the continuous action of variation and survival of the fittest, become so harmoniously adapted to plant life that it would inevitably have every *appearance* of the plant having been formed and preordained for the express purpose of sustaining and benefiting the animal.

So Wallace well understood that the co-adaptation of plant and animal life cannot be cited, of itself, as a proof of design. But neither was it any proof against it.[63]

Useful materials

Wallace spoke of the many different kinds of wood whose qualities – strength, lightness, ease of cutting, smoothness of surface, attractive appearance and durability – are so exactly suited to our needs that he thought it doubtful that we could have grown civilized without them.[64] He listed the seven 'ancient metals' as gold, silver, copper, iron, tin, lead and mercury. Though these metals, except iron, appeared to serve no important purpose either in the earth itself or for vegetables or animals, they had been of great importance in the development of civilization. He wondered why they were there.[65]

Carbon

In the second half of the nineteenth century, it became clear to scientists that organic substances – those derived directly or indirectly from living systems – all contained carbon. Organic molecules came to be defined as all those containing carbon. The exceptions are the simplest carbon compounds, carbon dioxide, chalk and other carbonates, for example, which are honorary inorganic compounds.

Carbon is the smallest atom, with has exactly four electrons in its outer shell so it can make four strong bonds at once. Carbon atoms are the basis of the molecules of life.

Wallace wrote about what he described as 'the mystery of carbon': the basis of organized matter and of life. He understood that the leaves of plants contained chlorophyll, which with the help of sunlight could extract carbon from carbon dioxide in the air. He was not aware of any other way this could be done at ordinary temperatures. Therefore he thought of carbon as perhaps the most distinctive of all the elements, and it seemed to him to exist for the one purpose of making the development of organized life possible.[66]

There is no doubt that the versatile combining powers of carbon, one of the elements flung into space during the explosion of dying stars, have played a central role in the origin of life. Indeed, we may think of ourselves as 'animated star dust'.

Wallace on water

Wallace noted that water was as essential for building up living organisms as was carbon. He wrote about the part water has played in modelling the earth's surface. Without water, life on earth would have been impossible. Water added to the beauty of the world. Another bonus in a world that seemed to Wallace to welcome humanity so warmly.[67]

When water begins to freeze, the water molecules orient themselves to maximize the special hydrogen bonding between molecules. This produces an open structure with large spaces in it, resulting in the density of ice being less than that of water. So ice floats. If it sank, like most solids do in their own liquid, in winter ice would form on the bottom of ponds, not at the top. The same would happen to the sea and instead of having ice as an insulating lid holding the remaining heat in, the oceans would lose all their heat and freeze solid, from the bottom up – and there'd be no life on earth. The inconvenience of the expansion of water in frozen pipes is a small price to pay for the environmental advantages of the decrease in density when water freezes!

And so, scientifically speaking, water is quite remarkable. I add, not only that water provides some of the most beautiful imagery in the Bible, but also that the fourth-century church father, Basil the Great, commenting on the Holy Spirit's activity in creation, remarked that 'the Spirit . . . prepared the nature of water to produce living beings'.[68]

Wallace on Darwin

Wallace insisted that Darwin always maintained that natural selection had been the most important but not the exclusive means of modification. In fact he took the line that he could advocate his own position without opposing Darwin, because the author of *The Origin* purposely excluded certain fundamental issues from his enquiries: the nature and causes of life itself and the powers of growth and reproduction.

Wallace always pointed to the 'laws of growth and reproduction' and of 'inheritance with variability' as being fundamental facts of nature without which natural selection would be powerless or even non-existent. He also took the view that these phenomena were beyond explanation or understanding. There is, says Wallace, a distinction between *representation* and *explanation*. In other words, the description of a process is not the same as its explanation. You have to account for the *forces*, the *directive* agency and the *organzing* power that are essential features of growth.[69]

Wallace on the wonder of birds

Wallace believed that birds were the most beautiful and wonderful of all living things. He expressed his admiration for them in evolutionary terms. If we were not so familiar with them, we would think it impossible that birds could have their forelimbs modified for flight. Birds are completely adapted to obtain every kind of food, to protect themselves from enemies, and to construct homes for their young. Their powers of flight are even more remarkable than insects. If you consider the weight they have to carry, the height at which they fly, their command over their direction and speed, and the complex organ by which they fly – the wing – birds win the prize. The insect's flight is simpler and more automatic, but the bird is more in control.

Although he spoke of the way the bird's wing had been 'adapted' for flight, it seemed to Wallace clearly to suggest the working out of a preconceived design which had produced a successful result. What, he asked, is the *constructive* power which welds cells together, in one place into solid bone, in another into muscle, in another into the light, strong, elastic material of the feather? What is the nature of the power that determines that every separate feather always grows into its exact shape? We are so familiar with the idea of 'growth' that we take it for granted.[70]

Certainly, today's biologists know much more than in the nineteenth century about the mechanical and molecular processes involved here and can provide perfectly good (if incomplete) descriptions of birds' wings and so on. My purpose is to emphasize that Wallace's pioneering understanding of natural selection led him in a quite different direction of thought from either Darwin or yourself.

Making life possible

Wallace listed the general conditions which he reckoned were essential for life on earth: light and heat from the sun; water universally distributed on the planet's surface and in the atmosphere; an atmosphere of sufficient density and composed of the several gases from which protoplasm can be formed; some alternation of light and darkness.

These indispensable conditions for life are met on earth. They have needed numerous, complex and exact adjustments to bring them about and maintain them almost unchanged throughout the millions of years during which life has developed. Other conditions that Wallace thought were essential for the maintenance of life – conditions which are all just right on earth – were the distance of the planet from the sun; the mass of the planet; the slant of the planet in its orbit; the amount of water as compared with land; the surface distribution of land and water; the permanence of this distribution dependent probably on the unique origin of our moon; an atmosphere of sufficient density and of suitable component gases; an adequate amount of dust in the atmosphere; and atmospheric electricity.[71]

On Wallace's point about the slant of the planet in its orbit, I understand that the earth's axis is tilted at 23.45 degrees relative to the plane of its orbit; and that our moon orbits the earth along its orbital plane while every other moon in the solar system orbits its planet around the equator. Although this phenomenon remains a mystery to astronomers, we do know that it is the only configuration that allows tides to exist on earth and that without them, life could not exist.

Darwin's distress

Darwin was distressed that Wallace rejected his conclusion that humanity's highest qualities evolved from animals by natural and sexual selection. When Wallace warned him that he was going to suggest for the first time some limitations to the power of natural selection, Darwin replied that he hoped Wallace had not 'murdered too completely your own and my child'.[72] Darwin told Sir Charles Lyell (1797–1875), the influential geologist, that he was 'dreadfully disappointed' in Wallace.[73]

Darwin wrote to Wallace: 'I differ grievously from you, and I am very sorry for it. I can see no necessity for calling in an additional and proximate cause in regard to Man. But the subject is too long for a letter.'[74] A few months later he wrote again to Wallace: 'I am very glad you are going to publish all your papers on Natural Selection: I am sure you are right, and that they will do our cause much good. But I groan over Man – you write like a metamorphosed (in retrograde direction) naturalist, and you the author of the best paper that ever appeared in the *Anthropological Review*! Eheu! Eheu! Eheu! – Your miserable friend, C. Darwin.'[75]

Wallace replied, 'I can quite comprehend your feelings with regard to my "unscientific" opinions as to Man, because a few years back I should myself have looked at them as equally wild and uncalled for.'[76]

Sir Charles Lyell continued to hold to the view that species could not change long after the publication of *The Origin of Species*, in fact until 1869. When he did bring himself to accept natural selection he preferred Wallace's version to Darwin's and wrote that:

> the Supreme Intelligence might possibly direct variation in a way analogous to that in which even the limited powers of man might guide it in selection, as in the case of the breeder and horticulturalist. In other words, as I feel that progressive development or evolution cannot be entirely explained by natural selection, I rather hail Wallace's suggestion that there may be a Supreme Will and Power which may not abdicate its functions of interference, but may guide the forces and laws of Nature.[77]

Wallace's spiritualism

Despite the honours which were showered upon him, and the quality and originality of his thought, you may be tempted to respond that Wallace was an eccentric. You and others will no doubt draw attention to his interest in spiritualism. This should be seen in context. The mid- to late nineteenth century saw an increasing interest in the afterlife as respectable people throughout England invited their friends into comfortable drawing rooms for séances. In part, this may have represented a feeling that there are more things in heaven and earth than scientists dreamt of. Coolly rational men like the Scottish publisher Robert Chambers, who with his brother founded *Chambers Encyclopaedia*, were persuaded that spiritualism should be investigated. After carefully noting the manifestations at a number of séances, Chambers decided that they 'compelled a reasonable man to believe in a spiritual agency, immortality and the hereafter'.[78]

Emma and Etty Darwin persuaded a reluctant Charles to go along to a séance arranged by his brother, the also sceptical Erasmus Darwin. George Eliot and her partner, George Henry Lewes, attended the party as well. According to Etty, Charles' daughter, 'the usual manifestations occurred: sparks, wind blowing and some rappings and moving of furniture'. Emma, who believed in an afterlife, did not dismiss spiritualism completely, although it never interested her greatly. Charles, however, grew irritated and left the stifling room, as he told the botanist Joseph Hooker, 'before all these astounding miracles, or jugglery, took place . . . the Lord have mercy on us all if we have to believe in such rubbish'.[79]

Wallace took spiritualism more seriously than Darwin, believing that the spiritual dimension to our existence should be scientifically analysed, even measured. After experiencing physical manifestations of tappings and rappings, table tiltings and levitations, names written on bits of paper, musical instruments spontaneously producing sounds, and, amazingly, the production of fruit and bunches of flowers, he grew convinced that there must be an unseen cause, a force which one could not explain away in conventional physical terms. Since he was aware that some mediums were frauds and that conjuring tricks were possible, he believed that careful systematic checks were required.

So he applied his own tests, secretly stretching thin tissue paper between table legs, constructing a cylinder of hoops and laths, covered with canvas, to protect the table from intruding feet or ladies' dresses. He produced an article, 'The Scientific Aspect of the Supernatural'.[80]

His argument in defence of spiritualism was that a number of intelligent, truthful people have experienced phenomena, which they believe cannot be explained away as coincidences. No doubt there is some trickery and some phenomena the authenticity of which is debatable. But many of those concerned are involved in good faith. He did not understand how it all worked, but one logical explanation fitted his scientific worldview: there is a 'higher' order of beings, of existence, in the universe. Certain people are able to put us in touch with that higher order.

He told other spiritualists that they should be fighting to reduce human misery.

> Let us demand Social Justice. This will be a work worthy of our cause, to which it will give dignity and importance. It will show our fellow-countrymen that we are not mere seekers after signs and wonders, mere interviewers of the lower denizens of the spirit-world; but that our faith, founded on knowledge, has a direct influence on our lives; that it teaches us to work strenuously for the elevation and permanent well-being of our fellow men.

Wallace and religion

Wallace's parents had been devout Anglicans taking him to church every Sunday to both morning and evening services. His father also had several Quaker and dissenting friends, which meant that Wallace also experienced non-conformist Christianity. However, as a young man he could find 'no sufficient basis of intelligible fact or connected reasoning to satisfy my intellect'[81] and when he left home he abandoned the practice of regular church-going. He hated theological dogmatism.

He was however, in 1858, welcomed to New Guinea by two German missionaries, whom he compared unfavourably to French Jesuits he had known in Singapore: 'Trading missionaries, teaching what Jesus said, but not doing as He did, can scarcely be expected to do more than give them [savage tribes] a very little of the superficial varnish of religion'[82] – implying that there was a depth of faith which was both genuine and valuable.

One of the grounds for his attacks on Haeckel was that the German zoologist was ignorant of the writings of the best thinkers in the churches.

The nearest we get to his understanding of God and creation is in a section of his book *The World of Life* where he deals with the relationship between science and religion.

> The main cause of the antagonism between religion and science seems to me to be the assumption by both that there are no existences capable of taking part in the work of creation other than blind forces on the one hand, and the infinite, eternal, omnipotent God on the other. The apparently gratuitous creation by theologians of angels and archangels, with no defined duties but that of attendants and messengers of the Deity, perhaps increases this antagonism, but it seems to me that both ideas are irrational. If, as I contend, *we are forced to the assumption of an infinite God by the fact that our earth has developed life and mind, and ourselves, it seems logical to assume that the vast, the infinite chasm between ourselves and the Deity is to some extent occupied by an almost infinite series of grades and beings, each successive grade having higher and higher powers in regard to the origination, the development, and the control of the universe* [my italics].[83]

These grades of beings are close to the 'principalities and powers' of which the Apostle Paul writes in his New Testament letters.

Following his death, aged ninety, in November 1913, the suggestion that Wallace should be buried in Westminster Abbey was turned down by his family. Instead he was buried in Broadstone cemetery in Dorset after a service conducted by the Bishop of Salisbury. It did not enter anyone's head that Wallace had solved the mystery of our existence in the sense of making atheism intellectually respectable.

Your forerunner

Ernst Haeckel is sometimes seen as the German equivalent of the British sociologist and philosopher Herbert Spencer (1820–1903), who was not only an early advocate of the theory of evolution but a believer in the preeminence of science over religion. If I were in a mood to make a further comparison, I would make the case for describing Haeckel as your forerunner. Haeckel (1834–1919) was the best-known German naturalist of his day, Professor of Zoology at Jena from 1862 until 1909. (I notice that your first degree was also in Zoology.) Haeckel popularized a materialistic philosophy, based on his Darwinism, and energetically sought to convince a whole generation of Germans that they should abandon their belief in God.

Haeckel began his crusade by offering a popular account of Darwin's new theory. But in areas where Darwin had been reticent, on the origins of humanity and on the initial creation, Haeckel was prepared to speak confidently. And he saw evolution as more than a biological theory.

For Haeckel, evolution was a whole way of picturing the world which removed the need for God. Actually – and maybe the comparison with you falls down a little here – Haeckel denied that he was a thoroughgoing materialist. Although he rejected any belief in humankind's having a distinct spirit or soul, he saw life and consciousness as built into the fabric of the universe. Even the simplest matter was not inert, but in some way possessed 'soul'. He even claimed that plants were conscious.

Like you, Haeckel believed that the development of the universe was a mechanical process without aim or purpose. What we call design in the living world is a special result of biological agencies. Neither in the path of the planets nor in the crust of the earth can we trace a controlling purpose. Everything is the result of chance. Our own human nature has no more value for the universe than an ant, 'the fly of a summer's day' or a tiny germ.

Opposition to Haeckel

Wallace had no time for Haeckel, believing his thinking was hopelessly muddled. The normally congenial and courteous Wallace dismissed Haeckel's views as vague, 'often incomprehensible assertions', 'improvable' and 'offensive to religious minds'. He accused Haeckel of being ignorant of the views of the best thinkers in the churches and criticized him for his dogmatism. While he was sympathetic to Haeckel's dislike of theological certainties, Wallace deplored his dogmatic rejection of a spiritual dimension and maintained that Haeckel was ignorant of the nature of life itself.[84]

Assessment of Wallace

No man who came up with the theory of natural selection independently of Darwin, but more quickly and almost effortlessly, can be described as a fool. If you compare the lists of the two men's writings, you are likely to conclude that the scope of Wallace's interests far outstripped those of Darwin.

Alfred Lord Tennyson, the poet, followed scientific ideas closely. Thomas Huxley commented that Tennyson's 'grasp of the principles of physical science was equal to that of the greatest experts'.[85] Wallace and Tennyson met once and the poet often spoke of Wallace's genius, being 'disposed to think his conclusions more exact in some respects than Darwin's'.[86]

You regularly link Wallace's name to your argument that evolution has solved the mystery of life and made atheism intellectually respectable. The reverse is the case: Wallace argued precisely the opposite. His view was that scientific observations led inevitably to belief in a higher being. It was not that he allowed God a role in those features of the world of life which he thought natural selection inadequate to explain; it was rather that all his observations of the universe in all its complex harmony suggested a 'benevolent author'. Once formed, he never budged from this view to the end of his life and this was for him the only explanation of humanity's special powers, morality and distinctive place in the universe. At the same time he continued to argue, write and lecture on all other aspects of Darwinian theory.

Wallace's view of God as a supreme intelligence preparing humanity for an enduring spiritual existence as the purpose of the universe is about as far away as possible from your bleak atheism. I agree with his biographer, Peter Raby, that,

Wallace would have been delighted by the clarity of genetics, but it is unlikely that genetics would have shaken his belief in a directive intelligence, which he expressed by these lines from Pope's 'Essay on Man':

All nature is but art unknown to thee;
All chance, direction which thou canst not see;
All discord, harmony not understood;
All partial evil, universal good.[87]

Human distinctiveness

In an article in *Free Inquiry* magazine, you wrote that Catholic morality is 'speciesist' to the core.

> You can kill adult animals for meat, but abortion and euthanasia are murder because *human* life is involved. Catholicism's 'net' is not limited to moral considerations, if only because Catholic morals have scientific implications. Catholic morality demands the presence of a great gulf between *Homo sapiens* and the rest of the animal kingdom. Such a gulf is fundamentally anti-evolutionary. The sudden injection of an immortal soul in the timeline is an anti-evolutionary intrusion into the domain of science.[88]

I am not a Catholic but I share the fundamentally Christian view that humanity is uniquely created in the image of God (which I consider later in this letter). The case for thinking of humans as occupying a special place in the animal kingdom rests on:

- the degree to which humans have developed language
- our fully reflective self-consciousness
- our use of imagination
- our ability to be creative
- our sense of absolute values
- our ability to choose between values
- our moral sense
- our philosophy, scientific theories and religious ideas.

Darwin was prepared to admit that there is an immense difference between 'the mind of the lowest man and that of the highest animal'. In an uncharacteristically imaginative passage in *The Descent of Man* he wrote:

An anthropomorphous ape [that is, allowing him for the moment to think like a human], if he could take a dispassionate view of his own case, would admit that though he could form an artful plan to plunder a garden – though he could use stones for fighting or for breaking open nuts, yet the thought of fashioning a stone into a tool was quite beyond his scope. Still less, as he would admit, could he follow out a train of metaphysical reasoning, or solve a mathematical problem, or reflect on God, or admire a grand natural scene. Some apes, however, would probably declare that they could and did admire the beauty of the coloured skin and fur of their partners in marriage (sic). They would admit that though they could make other apes understand by cries some of their perceptions and simpler wants, the notion of expressing definite ideas by definite sounds had never crossed their minds. They might insist that they were ready to aid their fellow-apes of the same troop in many ways, to risk their lives for them, and to take charge of their orphans, but they would be forced to acknowledge that disinterested love for all living creatures, the most noble attribute of man, was quite beyond their comprehension.[89]

However, Darwin insisted – and here he and Wallace could not agree – that 'the difference in mind between man and the higher animals, great as it is, certainly is one of degree and not of kind'.[90]

Later in this letter I shall note how Susan Greenfield thinks of 'mind' as the way humans build up a store of inner resources. Here, I observe that in the debate about human distinctiveness, Professor Greenfield seems to be more on the side of Wallace than Darwin when she writes: 'Humans spend far more time in these thinking and reasoning cognitive processes than any other mammal, even compared to our chimpanzee cousins, whose DNA is only 1 per cent different from our own. More than any other species, we can plan ahead, visualize a tool we might see as perfect for a certain task, form hopes about the future, and reflect on abstract concepts. Although the precise terminologies might vary, there is a unifying scheme: the generation of intellectual inner resources.'[91]

4

Evolution Today

For the benefit of non-scientist readers of this letter, Professor Dawkins, I should explain that all current biological research uses evolution as its working hypothesis. Evolution is understood at the level of deoxyribonucleic acid (DNA), the molecular carrier of hereditary information. The process of evolution involves the unfolding of diversity by the twin balancing effects of DNA mutations (tending to variation) and natural selection (acting against variation to preserve genes that work well). We all carry around in our bodies thousands of 'molecular fossils' – genes that are found in only slightly different forms in every living thing. If ever tempted to pride, we should remember that about 40 per cent of our genes are shared with fruit flies and worms!

The molecule of life, DNA, carries the information needed for the care and maintenance of an organism – whether the organism is a bacterium or a human being. Molecules of DNA are generally very long chains and are comprised of phosphate, a sugar, and four bases: adenine (A), guanine (G), thymine (T) and cystosine (C).

In the year that I write this letter, we celebrate the fiftieth anniversary of a remarkable breakthrough in 1953 by two researchers in Cambridge, Francis Crick and James Watson, which was to win them a Nobel Prize. They discovered that two chains of DNA twist around one another 'holding hands', with A always linking up with T, and C always linking up G, to make what became known as the 'double helix'. The sequence of letters along each chain store information in a message written with a four-letter alphabet.

There are two copies of each gene – the alleles – in each body cell, one copy of each autosomal chromosome of a matched pair. The sequence of bases along a specified strand of DNA contains the information for a gene that encodes the amino acid sequence of a protein, or part of a protein if it contains multiple sub-units. In turn proteins collaborate to build all the cells of the body.

The significance of the double helix

Opinions vary as to the implications of Watson and Crick's discovery. Commentators with a high view of the 1953 breakthrough argue that since that date we have understood that DNA is *the* molecule of heredity and that its structure holds the key to the understanding of heredity's molecular mechanism. DNA is just a chemical substance, yet is more than just a large molecule. By virtue of its chemical nature, DNA is an information store. Since 1953, say the enthusiasts, we have come to understand how genes are built up, and how, within them, the transition from inanimate matter to the 'blueprint of life' takes place.

Critics of biological determinism have argued that the new insights into DNA's information-bearing qualities still leave unanswered all sorts of questions about the information in both DNA and proteins. Does not natural selection presuppose a pre-existing mechanism of self-replication? The whole mechanism needs information, but where does it come from?

More generally it has been pointed out that DNA does not produce life itself. We can certainly regard it as the source code that the cell reads in order to manufacture proteins that are, in turn, used as the bricks and mortar and metabolic machinery of the living world. But this fact contributes virtually nothing to solving the problem of how the living organism is actually assembled in all its structural and functional complexity from these basic molecular building blocks. The entire process gives the appearance of being goal-centred. The cell seems intent on producing a particular protein for a particular task. It is the total integrated system that gets things done, not DNA as a kind of 'molecular maestro' (the phrase was coined by Neil Broom).[92]

Returning to your own work, Professor Dawkins, you are firmly in the enthusiasts' camp, and are at your most ecstatic when you write about the implications of Crick and Watson's discovery. You call it a 'digital revolution at the very core of life'.[93] You use the term 'digital' because the information is expressed in pairs of letters. Up until 1953, you say, it was still possible to believe that there was something fundamentally and irreducibly mysterious in living protoplasm – but no longer.

'There's no spirit-driven life force,' you say. 'Life is just bytes and bytes and bytes of digital information. All living things, including ourselves, are survival machines programmed to propagate the digital database that did the programming. Darwinism has been refined. It is now understood as the survival of the survivors at the level of pure, digital code.'[94]

But Steve Rose, the biologist and author, is scathing. He says that you may regard yourself as nothing but a digital PC, and your complex lifeline in space and time as the read-out from a one-dimensional string of As and Cs and Gs and Ts, but things are more complicated than this. Rose points out that organisms are not passive responders to their environments. They actively choose to change them, and to work to that end. Your interpretation of natural selection implies that organisms are the mere playthings of fate, sandwiched between their genetic endowment and an environment over which they have no control, which is constantly setting their genes challenges that they can either pass or fail. Organisms, however, are far from passive: they – not just we humans, but all other living forms as well – are active players in their own futures.[95]

Self-replication

You told one interviewer that, while you have little patience with theologians, you love the study of biblical literature.[96] Your books have as many biblical allusions as mine. In *The Blind Watchmaker*, you recall Ezekiel calling on the four winds to put living breath into the dry bones. You ask 'What is the vital ingredient that a dead planet like the early Earth must have, if it is to have a chance of eventually coming alive, as our planet did?' It is not breath, you reply, nor wind, nor elixir nor potion. It is not a substance at all; it is a property: the property of self-replication. This is the basic ingredient of cumulative selection.

You point out that if anything anywhere has the property of being good at making more copies of itself, then automatically more and more copies of that entity will come into existence. Cumulative selection cannot work unless there is some minimal machinery of replication and replicator power. You frankly admit that you do not know how replication machinery came into existence but you refuse to put it down to a supernatural designer. You think that would explain nothing, for it would simply beg the question about the origin of the designer.[97] I talk in section 9 of this letter both about the origin of the designer and what we mean when we say that replication is an 'automatic process'.

'Survival machines'

You have described an individual animal or human body as a large vehicle or 'survival machine' built by a gene co-operative for the preservation of copies of each member of that co-operative. They co-operate because they all stand to gain from the same outcome – the survival and reproduction of the communal body.

Your use of the word 'co-operate' sounds suspiciously purposeful for a so-called blind process. Indeed, in your description of what goes on genetically, you constantly use the language of analogy. In the process you attribute to genes human characteristics. I imagine you defend this practice by saying that it aids understanding especially for the non-specialist. The cost, however, is a loss in clarity and precision of thought. For example, having told us about the so-called 'genetic dictionary' with its 64 DNA words, you go on to argue that, at the level of genes, every living thing 'speaks' almost exactly the same language. So we have genes speaking, building and co-operating.

You speak of surviving replicators – genes – building survival machines for themselves to live in. Survival machines got bigger and more elaborate. And then, in a famous and controversial passage in *The Selfish Gene*, you say: 'Now they swarm in huge colonies, safe inside gigantic lumbering robots, sealed off from the outside world, communicating with it by tortuous indirect routes, manipulating it by remote control. They are in you and me; they created us, body and mind; and their preservation is the ultimate rationale for our existence. They have come a long way, those replicators. Now they go by the name of genes, and we are their survival machines.'[98]

Genetic determinism

When these sentences appeared in *The Selfish Gene*, you were accused of 'genetic determinism'. In a footnote to a later edition of your book, you admitted that this was one of your 'purple passages' but you were quite unrepentant about using the word 'robot'. 'What on earth do you think you are if you are not a robot?' you asked.

Steve Rose took issue with you over your use of the term 'survival machines'. He accused you of having the 'brash style of a cheeky adolescent cocking a snook at everything his elders hold dear' and being 'the St John the Baptist of socio-biology' who writes 'in the comfort of an Oxford college'. He considers your books to be more an exercise of political sloganeering than advancing a sustainable philosophical position.

Humans, says Rose, are like, yet unlike, any other species on earth. We are not reducible to 'nothing but' machines for the replication of our DNA. Humans are active in shaping their own pathways through life.[99]

Rose is by no means alone in attacking the whole idea of genetic determinism. Richard Lewontin has argued that the very idea of the gene being the molecular mastermind behind all living things is scientifically and conceptually flawed. Portraying genes as having the ability to produce proteins and make copies of themselves endows them with what Lewontin calls 'a mysterious, autonomous power that seems to place them above the more ordinary materials of the body'. But these notions actually explain little about the real nature of life itself and how it might have arisen in the first place.[100]

Reductionism

You are often accused of reductionism and when the subject came up at a *Guardian* debate to which I refer later in this letter you said: 'Reductionism is one of those words that makes me want to reach for my revolver. It means nothing. Or rather it means a whole lot of different things, but the only thing anybody knows about it is that it's bad and you're supposed to disapprove of it.'[101]

This was a characteristically robust but somewhat emotional response. A more measured approach would be to distinguish between two types of reductionism. The first, 'methodological reductionism', is a research strategy absolutely essential in the pursuit of science involving taking a system apart and analysing the properties of components individually so that they can be understood in isolation before studying how they interact. The second, 'ontological reductionism' (*ontology* being the study of existence or being), also sometimes known as 'nothing buttery', is the type of thinking which says that humans are nothing but machines for propagating DNA or that the sounds created by violins are nothing but vibrations of a certain wavelength in the air.

I leave you to decide whether you may not at times be guilty of the second type of reductionism. Please leave your revolver in your drawer.

5

What Evolution Explains

In an interview you gave to the British Humanist Association, published in September 2002, you talked about the early influences that led you to study science. You said that your father read botany at Oxford, and had a scientific attitude, which rubbed off on you. You told your interviewer:

> I more or less drifted into the biological stream in the sixth form but was more interested in the philosophical aspects of science, in particular evolution. What was important about evolution was that it explained our existence and everything about our existence, and I suppose you could say that that impinges upon the same territory that religion does. My negativity towards religion began when I was quite a young child, but I finally lost my religious beliefs at the age of about sixteen, once I understood the full power of evolution by natural selection as the explanation for all of living complexity.[102]

The nature of our world

When Sheena McDonald interviewed you for Channel 4 in 1994, you told her that you loved your life and all sorts of aspects of it that had nothing to do with your science. You said that neither your own feelings nor the world itself were cold and bleak. You thought of the world as a lovely and a friendly place which you enjoyed being in.

But you have also asserted that there is no logical reason why we should try to derive our normative standards from evolution. You think it perfectly consistent to say on the one hand that natural selection is out there and is a very unpleasant process – nature is red in tooth and claw – and that on the other hand you do not want to live in that kind of a world. You want to change the world in which you live in such a way that natural selection no longer applies.

Apart from your misleading portrayal of natural selection as, in Tennyson's words, 'red in tooth and claw' – 'survival of the fittest' rarely involves battles to the death between individual animals, but rather struggling with a harsh environment – I am not sure that you have understood the tensions inherent in your position here. To the extent that we do find unpleasantness, how do you account for your admirable desire to fight against Darwinism to change the world and make it a better place?

What is chance?

In the minds of many people, there are two possible explanations for our existence: either we are created by God or we are here by chance. On my website (details at the end of this letter) I have published a fairly detailed summary of Jacques Monod's ideas about *Chance and Necessity*. For Monod, the secret of life was chance, as he put it in *Chance and Necessity*, 'random chance caught on the wing, preserved, reproduced by the molecular machinery of invariance and thus converted into order, rule, necessity'.[103] Was Monod right to translate the behaviour of molecules into a philosophical principle in interpreting the universe?

To answer this question, we need to reflect on what we mean by chance. Chance does not make things happen or *do* anything: rather it is a description of the way in which we as observers understand the workings of events in the world around us (and we may describe events as happening by chance because *in practice* we are unable accurately to predict the outcome – such as when we toss a coin – or because an outcome cannot *in principle* be predicted as in the case of the conventional understanding of quantum mechanics).

Monod carefully described the behaviour of molecules within living things and characterized this as being according to chance. He went on from there to insist that we live in a universe which is governed by 'chance and necessity' and certainly not by some overall plan or by a Creator. However, when we think of the way that matter behaves on a larger scale, we see that there are many regularities, which we call laws, that arise from the combined effects of 'random' microscopic events.

But take the so-called random molecular events in DNA. These events occur in a system which has the properties it has because its constituent atoms and molecules have *their* characteristic properties. You could say that the emergence of the immense variety of living forms manifests the potentialities of matter. This happens, in a sense, as all the available possibilities of matter are explored in the course of random molecular events – for example when proteins 'recognize' each other (in the way Monod described) – but in many other ways throughout the universe.

Your own position is that there is an element of chance in the way matter behaves in the process of natural selection, but that it is not mostly chance. You characterize it as a whole series of small chance steps. In order, you say, for an eye to evolve, each eye along the evolutionary journey is a little bit better than the one before, but each step is not so great that it is unbelievable that it could have come about by chance. At the end of a long period of non-random natural selection, you have accumulated lots and lots of these steps, although the end product is far too improbable to have come about in a single step of chance.

But whether one is happy, as Monod was, to use the word 'chance', or whether one prefers, like you, to put the stress on 'non-random survival', does this justify taking the mechanistic view of our existence which both you and Monod have adopted? Why should the mechanisms described by molecular biology tell us anything about ultimate questions of meaning?

We surely have to account for the remarkable fact that the most significant of the properties of matter is that, organized in certain ways over an immensely long period, it produces the characteristics we call living and, indeed, human too. The primeval cloud of gas, or soup, whatever it was, has developed into living organisms and then into people, with all their qualities, achievements and potential for good and evil.

If everything is the result, as Monod tries to argue, of chance and necessity in the motion of the molecules out of which the world is constructed, it would follow that any one individual must be entirely conditioned by the motion of the molecules out of which he is constructed. Similarly another individual who had opposite views would have to be understood as developing and pronouncing such views only through chance and necessity similarly operating. The collision of views between these two individuals would consist in nothing other than the collision of the two sets of active molecules out of which they were constructed.

This would lead to an utter impasse, for the individual who claimed that all was mechanical would have to assert that his views were true while his opponent's views were false. But on that view of the universe what is the origin of concepts like 'truth' and 'falsehood'? The holder of the mechanistic view would have to imply that the opponent who consistently failed to agree with him must have somehow been deceiving himself. But what can it mean for a machine to deceive itself? And what can it mean for one machine to say that it knows that it is functioning correctly to give the truth, while it knows that another similar machine functions falsely?

Consider an honest gambling casino – assuming for a moment there is such a thing. The rolling of dice or shuffling of cards leads to an authentically random result. But the operators of the casino purposefully employ and depend on that very randomness in their calculation of payoff rates to ensure that the place will make a handsome profit. Now, if we as humans are able to employ random processes to accomplish our purposes, could not the Creator do the same on a far grander scale? Instead of jumping hastily, as Monod did, from the recognition of random molecular variations to the conclusion of ultimate purposelessness, could it be that these 'random' variations are God's way to achieve his purposes for the world he created?

You prefer not to use the word 'random' and stress that cumulative natural selection works according to a well-understood principle. That said, although you avoid using the word 'random', you do assert that the whole evolutionary process of natural selection is 'blind' and without overall meaning and purpose. Somewhat confusingly, however, you do acknowledge that there has been 'progress' from simplicity to complexity.

Denis Alexander reminds us that:

> the fact that any mechanism per se is by definition 'mindless' does not exclude the possibility that it has a meaning and purpose defined by its incorporation into the larger scheme of things. The fact that the operation of pistons, spark plugs and carburettors in a car engine are 'mindless' does not imply that

the car-driver has no chosen destination. The fact that the various mechanisms that comprise the operating parts of jet engines are 'mindless' has no implications for the existence of Frank Whittle who originally designed the jet engine.[104]

Natural selection does not operate in a vacuum

In any given environment, carbon-based life can only have so many properties. During the billions of years over which living things have evolved, the potentialities of matter have been fully explored within constraints imposed by food, gravity, the composition of the gases in the atmosphere and the sun's heat and light. Remove the sun and we would all be dead. These constraints within which natural selection has operated have channelled life forms within certain ordered parameters. In addition there have been less ordered and some highly unpredictable constraints such as climate changes, volcanoes and meteorites wiping out dinosaurs.

Incidentally the fact that both we ourselves and the process of natural selection depend on the sun does not imply that the details or direction of biological diversity are *programmed* by the sun. In that sense, the sun may be a helpful (though imperfect) analogy for the Creator. We depend on him for our life, but he gives us autonomy – and free will.

What you refer to as the 'well-understood' parameters within which natural selection operates assume the reliability of the laws of physics and chemistry (which in any case imply a lawgiver) as well as biological processes such as 'growth' which are not included in the description of natural selection. There can be no doubt that the results of the whole process are remarkable, giving every impression of design and purpose.

The universe as an expression of God's will

Howard Van Till is a retired American Professor of Physics and Astronomy who is also committed to the historic Christian doctrine of creation. He sees the entire universe – every atom, every physical structure, every living organism – as a creation that has only been an expression of God's effective will. God is the universe's Creator in the fundamental sense of being the One who has given the universe its being. The being of the universe is radically dependent on the effective will of its Creator.

According to Van Till, essential to the being of creation is not only a set of properties that characterize its many substances, structures and organisms, but also a vast array of creaturely capabilities for action and interaction, including capabilities for self-organization and transformation. Quarks, for instance, possess the capabilities to interact in such a way as to form protons and neutrons – nucleons. Nucleons, in turn, have the capacities to interact and organize, by such processes as thermonuclear fusion, into progressively larger atomic nuclei. Nuclei and electrons have the capability to interact and organize into atoms. On the macroscopic scale, vast collections of atoms interact to form the inanimate structures of galaxies, stars and planets. On the microscopic scale, atoms interact chemically to form molecules; molecules interact to form more complex molecules. Some molecular ensembles apparently possess the capabilities to organize into the fundamental units that constitute living cells and organisms.[105]

Humans are apparently the outcome of the cosmic evolution of matter. From the 'stuff of the world', some chemical reactions within matter have become humanity. After millions of years, matter has turned into men and women, atoms have become human beings, aware of themselves.

Human identity: Who are you?

In February 1995, Nick Pollard interviewed you in your rooms near New College in Oxford. During the course of the interview your wife, Lalla, made a pot of tea. Nick pointed out that if he asked, 'Why is that kettle boiling?' you could have had a conversation about processes or you could have considered another meaning of 'why', which is to do with purpose. The reason the kettle was boiling was that your wife had put the kettle on to make a cup of tea.

You suggested that the explanation that somebody switched on the kettle and had a purpose in doing so was simply a more complicated problem that now had to be solved. 'We now have to go and look at her brain and ask what it is that made her want to switch the kettle on. And that takes us back to the workings of her brain, to why she has a brain in the first place, which gets us back to evolution. There's a whole cascade of similar explanations.'

At this point Nick asked you whether you were not explaining your wife away.

'Who is she?' he asked.

'Well, that's a more profound question,' you replied. 'What is a human? What is a human self, a human individual? That's more difficult. It's not a question I can answer – it's not a question any scientist can answer at present, though I think they will. I believe it will turn out that what a human is is some manifestation of brain stuff and its workings.'

Nick then quoted Dr Susan Blackmore, a psychologist with an interest in evolutionary theory and consciousness, who had recently told *The Skeptic* magazine: 'I think the idea we exist is an illusion . . . The idea that there is a self in there that decides things, acts and is responsible . . . is a whopping great illusion. The self we construct is just an illusion because actually there's only brains and chemicals and this "self" doesn't exist – it never did and there's nobody to die.'

When Nick asked whether you agreed with this, you replied: 'Yes. I mean, Susan is sticking her neck out for one particular view of what a self is, and it's one that I am inclined to think is probably right; but I don't think we are yet in a position to substantiate that. What makes it seem plausible to me is various things. One is that brains have come into the world by a gradual process of evolution and we have a continuum from ourselves through all the other animals to animals that have very simple brains, to animals that have no brains at all, to plants . . .'

Nick then asked you whether you believed that the idea that he existed was an illusion. You replied: 'Well, I'm certainly happy that we are a product of brains and that when our brains die, we disappear. To call us an illusion is possibly a good way to express it. But I wouldn't wish to commit myself to saying that our sense of self is an illusion. It depends what you mean. I certainly feel that there's a me.'

At another time you said that, as a Darwinian, you felt mystified by your own niceness. You think we are nicer than a Darwinian explanation would lead us to expect.

Well, it could be that your niceness is explained because we are all created in the image of God. As a result of something that I know you do not believe in – the Fall – your niceness, like mine, at times wears a little thin. So we are a rather complex and unpredictable mixture of niceness and nastiness. I know this does not impress you. But I rather think you struggle to deal with issues of human identity.

Our sense of purpose

In *River out of Eden* you wrote: 'In a universe of blind physical forces and genetic replication, some people are going to get hurt, other people are going to get lucky, and you won't find any rhyme or reason in it, nor any justice. The universe we observe has precisely the properties we should expect if there is, at bottom, no design, no purpose, no evil and no good, nothing but blind, pitiless indifference.'[106]

Even if our rationale is simply to preserve our genes, that surely is to admit that there is some purpose in our being here. You are adamant that there is no purpose among genes: 'The replicators are no more conscious or purposeful than they ever were. The same old processes of automatic selection between rival molecules by reasons of their longevity, fecundity, and copying-fidelity, still go on as blindly and as inevitably as they did in far-off days. Genes have no foresight. They do not plan ahead. Genes just *are*, some genes more so than others, and that is all there is to it.'[107]

And yet you concluded your Dimbleby lecture by conceding that people feel the 'need' for something more in their lives than just the material world. There is a gap that must be filled. People need to feel a sense of purpose. You suggested that finding out what is already here, in the material world, before concluding that we need something more would not be bad for a start. You asked how much more people want than a sense of wonder at the world about them. True science, you say, is well qualified to feed this sense of wonder. 'Just study what is,' you said, 'and you'll find that it already is far more uplifting than anything you could imagine needing.'

You have said that you want to guard against people getting nihilistic in their personal lives. You see no reason for that. You think it is possible to have a happy and fulfilled personal life even if the universe at large is a tale told by an idiot. We can still set up goals and have a worthwhile life.

Your honest admission that people feel this need of a sense of purpose, which you want to encourage, does beg the question as to how these goals get implanted in our minds in a world for which evolution by natural selection is a sufficient explanation of our existence.

Why are we here?

Darwin and Wallace set out to solve the mystery of biological diversity. They came up with the theory of evolution by natural selection. It was a major insight in the progress of scientific understanding. However, you go on to make an unjustified leap in claiming that they solved the mystery of our existence – implying that it is an explanation that answers all our questions about life and the universe. This leap gets you into trouble.

When you were being interviewed on American television for the *Think Tank* series, Ben Wattenberg put it to you that Darwin does not really answer the question why we are here. Maybe Darwin helps us understand *how* we are here, but Wattenberg suggested to you that when most people ask the question 'Why are we here?' they expect a theological or religious answer. 'Does Darwin really talk about why we are here in that sense?' he asked. You replied: 'Darwin, if I may say so, had better things to do than talk about why we are here in that sense. It's not a sensible sense in which to ask the question. There's no reason why, just because it's possible to ask the question, it's necessarily a sensible question to ask.'

Very reasonably, being obviously a smart man and well prepared for his interview, Mr Wattenberg was not going to let you get away with that. He pointed out that earlier in the interview you had made the point that, after many centuries of human questioning, Darwin had told us why we are here.

You seem to have struggled at this point and said, 'I was using "why" in another sense. I was using "why" in the sense of the explanation, and that's the only sense which I think is actually a legitimate one. I don't think the question of ultimate purpose, the question of what is the fundamental purpose for which the universe came into existence – I believe there isn't one. If you asked me what '.... Wattenberg intervened to check that you were actually saying that you did not believe there is a purpose to the universe. You confirmed that you do not think the universe has a purpose and continued:

> On the other hand, if you ask me, what is the purpose of a bird's wing, then I'm quite happy to say, well, in the special Darwinian sense, the purpose of a bird's wing is to help it fly, therefore to survive and therefore to reproduce the genes that gave it those wings that make it fly. Now, I'm happy with that meaning of the word 'why'. But the ultimate meaning of the word 'why' I do not regard as a legitimate question. And the mere fact that it's possible to ask the question doesn't make it legitimate. There are plenty of questions I could imagine somebody asking me and I wouldn't attempt to answer it. I would just say, 'That's a silly question, don't ask it.'

Wattenberg scented a little victory here and responded quietly, 'So you are not only saying that religious people are coming to a wrong conclusion. You are saying they're asking a silly question.'

You had no alternative but to agree that you were indeed saying that.[108]

Now, I do not want to appear to be gloating, but I must say that I think readers of this letter will find this exchange extraordinary in at least two respects. First, here you are, you have been appointed as Professor of the Public Understanding of Science in one of the most ancient universities in the world. Over the centuries at Oxford, students have been encouraged to ask and develop answers to all sorts of questions: mathematical, scientific, philosophical, historical and theological. Indeed, for much of its history, every teacher at the university was also ordained in the service of God. And now you come along and tell us that ultimate questions about why we are here are not only illegitimate but silly.

Second, you cannot have it both ways. You cannot tell us at one moment that Darwin and Wallace 'solved the mystery of our existence' and then go on to tell us that we must not ask ultimate questions about the purpose of the universe.

Apparent purposefulness of evolution

Roger Penrose, the distinguished Oxford mathematician who has received prizes for his work with Stephen Hawking in developing our understanding of the universe, thinks that there is something mysterious about evolution, with its apparent 'groping' towards some future purpose. He thinks things seem to organize themselves rather better than they ought to, just on the basis of natural selection. He speculates that there is something about the way the laws of physics work, which allows natural selection to be a much more effective process than it would be with just arbitrary laws. This apparently 'intelligent groping' is an intriguing issue, which I do not think you and other atheistic biologists satisfactorily answer.[109]

I think the explanation has to do with the potentialities with which God has endowed matter and his moment by moment involvement in the unfolding process of nature. I talk later in this letter about how Christians understand 'nature'.

Life's improbability

Despite the vehemence of your attacks on Christianity and repeated descriptions of all religion as a virus, I warm to your honesty. For example, I love your frank admission in *The Blind Watchmaker* that life is a huge statistical improbability. You point out that it would be no good taking the right number of atoms and shaking them together with some external energy like the sun until they happen to fall into the right pattern, and expecting Adam to drop out! A human consists of over a thousand million million million million atoms. You say that to try to make a man, we would have to work at a biochemical cocktail-shaker for a period so long that the entire age of the universe would seem like an eye-blink, and even then we would not succeed.

You make this point as an introduction to your description of how cumulative natural selection has, over the enormity of geological time, produced not only humans but the diversity of life we see around us.

But there is another category of your honesty to which I want to draw attention. This consists of areas where you frankly admit that Darwinism does not provide us with either a complete or satisfactory understanding of various phenomena. And please note what I am saying here: I am by no means clinging to the hope that these will continue to constitute areas of ignorance which will remain the preserve of God. I have no doubt that our understanding will increase and that this will go hand in hand with a strengthening of our sense of wonder at the complexity of the world around us and the believer's sense of awe at the greatness of the Creator. My point is that these admissions do not sit happily with your claim that Darwin and Wallace solved the mystery of our existence.

How natural selection got started: the origin of life

You admit that evolution by natural selection could not have kick-started itself. It could not have started until there was some kind of rudimentary reproduction and heredity. Modern heredity is based on the DNA code, which is too complicated to have sprung spontaneously into being by a single act of chance. There must have been some earlier hereditary system, now disappeared, which was simple enough to have arisen – according to your worldview – by chance and the laws of chemistry, and which provided the medium in which a primitive form of cumulative natural selection could get started. DNA was a later product of this earlier cumulative selection. You do not tell us how you account for the 'laws of chemistry': laws normally imply a lawgiver.

Before natural selection got going there was a period when complex chemical compounds were built up from simpler ones and before that a period when the chemical elements were built up from simpler constituents, following what you describe as 'well-understood laws of physics'. Once again you do not account for the reliability and predictability over millions of years of these laws of physics and their apparent uniformity throughout the universe. I think you also need to give us some account of why you think there is a universe rather than *no universe*. You may say that is not a sensible question, or a question for a zoologist, but it is a question which arises because of your wide-ranging assertion that God is improbable and unnecessary.

You know that the origin of life must have been something which was self-replicating. The first replicator – something which can make a copy of itself – had to arrive on the scene. It had to be able to grow and split and then produce daughter units like itself. And then we get mutations, two or more different types of self-replicating molecules in a state of Darwinian competition.

In an interview with *The Skeptic* magazine you said that you would have to be more of a chemist than you are to know how probable it is that such molecules are actually likely to emerge. You suggested that chemists should divert more research effort 'toward devising an alternative hypothetical chemistry that supports self-replication, a whole alternative system that could, in principle, give rise to life. The fundamental principle that will be required is self-replication . . . I don't know how difficult it would be to achieve that chemically.'[110] We shall all watch with interest progress in 'template' chemistry research. You have said that there are various theories as to how life may have originated but that none of them is fully convincing. You note that it may be that none of them ever will be because we may never know what the conditions were. It was, after all, rather a long time ago.

Many scientists believe that life began in an atmosphere without oxygen, and the first self-replicating molecules were RNA, a nucleic acid similar to DNA. They think that the common ancestor of all life probably used RNA as its genetic material. No such replicator has yet been discovered. However, at the Scripps Research Institute in California they are working on the problem using computer simulations, which Gerald Joyce described in the journal *Nature* for 21 November 2002.

My point here is that your understandable uncertainty about precisely how life began sits oddly with your bold assertion that the mystery of our existence has been solved. The origin of life itself is by definition a fundamental ingredient of the understanding of our existence. If I say that I believe, as I do, that God is the author of life, that does not imply a fear on my part that scientists may gain new insights into the origin of life and how the process of natural selection began. Such advances in our understanding would, I suggest, have no more implication for religious belief than did Newton's insights into gravity – except perhaps to deepen faith as they did for Newton himself and for Robert Boyle when he pioneered our knowledge of the properties of gases and Johannes Kepler when he constructed a better orbital theory for Mars. Kepler's reaction to his own insight, as he told Galileo, was to be filled with a 'surging love of God'.[111]

The fun of making babies

You admit that sex is a problem for those who see Darwinism as a sufficient explanation of our existence. With humans there is no problem in seeing why sexual desire has Darwinian survival value. Anybody can see that. However, you say, greenflies and elm trees don't 'do it', and yet there are plenty of them around; why do the rest of us go to such lengths to mix our genes up with somebody else's before we make a baby? You acknowledge that it is an odd way to proceed – a 'bizarre perversion of straightforward replication', 'an inefficient way for an individual to propagate genes'.[112]

It is odd that we cannot yet fit the phenomenon of sex – which is said to figure so prominently in the everyday thinking of most humans and without which none of our contemporaries would be here – into our understanding of evolution. As you say, the pure survival value of sex is obvious: but why do we have the bonus of enjoying it so much? It would not be nearly so odd if you could bring yourself to consider the possibility that sex is given us by the Creator as a good gift. No doubt biologists will make progress in explaining the reason for sex. Christians will see this explanation, together with the ultimate purposes of God in creating human love and sex, as complementary understandings.

6

The Mind's Complexity

Galileo wrote: 'When I consider what marvellous things and how many of them men have understood . . . I recognize and understand only too clearly that the human mind is a work of God's and one of the most excellent.'[113] And Pascal, the seventeenth-century French mathematician, physicist and religious philosopher said: 'All bodies, the firmament, the stars, the earth and its kingdoms are not worth the least of minds, for it knows them all and itself too, while bodies know nothing.' The mind is a marvellous laboratory in which both to test hypotheses and to demonstrate the nature of complexity because it is accessible to all of us for research purposes.

Consider how well the mind performs in everyday situations. You and every reader of this letter can analyse what you are reading, agree with what you believe to be true, reject what you know to be false, doubt any overstatement, warm to that which rings true to your experience. You may be forming subtle judgements about the quality of my writing, the nuances of my standpoint, the originality of my insight, the profundity or otherwise of my thought. You may feel that at times you can 'read between the lines'.

Your perception is that you are free to put the letter down and listen instead while your wife reads you a poem. Let us imagine that Lalla enters the room but you know intuitively that she is not in the mood for reading aloud. You choose instead to take a walk and become enchanted by the beauty of the evening as the sun sets beyond the dreaming spires of Oxford. You meet an old friend and something in his features suggests that he has grown in grace and charm since last you met. The intelligent sparkle in his eyes brings back memories of congenial evenings long ago over a pint at *The Trout*.

'I've just read a biography of the late Cardinal Basil Hume,' he tells you. 'It was a joy to read. I was struck by his quality of unselfconscious holiness – God rest his soul. What precisely are the survival advantages of holiness, old man?'

He laughs and thumps you heartily on the back. You reflect that your initial impressions of a newfound charm were premature.

You return to your home. Lalla has picked up an open copy of *The Merchant of Venice* you have been reading prior to a visit to Stratford. You detect that her mood has changed and you persuade her to read Portia's words:

> The quality of mercy is not strain'd.
> It droppeth as the gentle rain from heaven
> Upon the place beneath: it is twice bless'd;
> It blesseth him that gives, and him that takes.
> 'T is mightiest in the mightiest, it becomes
> The throned monarch better than his crown:
> His sceptre shows the force of temporal power,
> The attribute to awe and majesty,
> Wherein doth sit the dread and fear of kings;
> But mercy is above this sceptred sway,
> It is enthroned in the heart of kings,
> It is an attribute to God himself,
> And earthly power doth then show likest God's,
> When mercy seasons justice.

Your thoughts wonder: *Does anyone read aloud more enchantingly than Lalla and yet so modestly? What was the secret of Shakespeare's genius? Was he born with it? Did he work at it? Was it a combination of nature and nurture? From whom did he learn such wisdom? Where did he gain his understanding of human nature? Why did he spoil his majestic prose by smuggling God in? What is justice? What is mercy? How do evolutionary psychologists explain it? Oh, even I wish that they wouldn't try to interpret everything in Darwinian terms . . .*

You feel a little creative yourself: will you write a letter to Juliet, continue constructing a chapter of your latest book, prepare a candle-lit supper for two, cook a meal or sketch a picture entitled 'Sunset in Oxfordshire'? Before you can write, cook or paint imaginatively you need ideas – but you are hopeful that the muse is on you. To assist the process you play a CD of Hadyn's *Te Deum*. The sound is glorious, inspirational – but, in reflective mood, you idly ask yourself 'What is glory?' 'What does it mean to be inspired?' The CD ends and, on the radio, you hear a news bulletin which reports a speech by President Bush in which he has spoken of a continuing international battle between good and evil – but, he assures you 'good will prevail'. As a materialistic atheist, you ask yourself how the President is going to identify what is good and what is evil and how can he be so sure that one will prevail over the other? What is goodness? How can he be so confident of what is right and what is wrong?

The next day is the first day of a new year. You make a resolution to live a more disciplined life, to be more organized in your reading, more discriminating in your TV viewing and spend more time with your family. You will aim to be a kinder, more considerate person. Your conscience tells you it is time you visited an elderly relative, give to Oxfam or join a demonstration protesting against the level of student debt or cruelty to animals.

As the months pass, you are aware of a growth and deepening of your personality, a sense of integrity, of emotional depth, that you're 'getting it together'. Your character is maturing. You feel you can draw on an inner strength. You are going through a process of self-discovery. Life is somehow more meaningful. You have regained your sense of dignity and moral purpose.

In your less worthy moods, however (if you are anything like me), you are aware of your capacity to manipulate people, to be irresponsible, untrustworthy, hypocritical, selfish. After a succession of selfish acts your conscience troubles you to the extent that you lose sleep and cannot face your food. Although you would love to feel at peace again, you experience the annoying sensation of 'being unable to forgive yourself' – an uninvited sense of self-loathing. You long to hear yourself laugh spontaneously again, enjoying the delights of a sense of humour, regaining your self-respect. As you experience this vast, almost infinite, range of emotions you feel that there are some that you are able to summon at will whereas others are tiresomely beyond your control.

In the course of a dozen paragraphs where I'm afraid I've let my imagination run riot, I have used some fifty words which represent abstract concepts with which the mind is at home: awareness, beauty, character, charm, conscience, cruelty, dignity, emotions, emotional depth, evil, fear, forgiveness, glory, good, goodness, grace, growth (of personality), happiness, holiness, hope, humour, hypocrisy, ideas, inner strength, insight, inspiration, integrity, intelligence, intuition, joy, judgement, kindness, loathing, meaning, mercy, modesty, morality, perception, pleasure, profundity, right, self-discovery, self-esteem, self-respect, senses, soul, spirit, strength of purpose, understanding, wisdom and wrong.

Whence this awareness?

According to your worldview this capacity of the human brain to handle with ease a vast range of emotions has evolved from mindless matter over many millions of years by a process of cumulative natural selection. That is all there is to it. There is no Creator who created matter with all its potential for evolution; who wills that matter should continue to have such properties; who is the giver of the laws of physics and chemistry; and who sustains us moment by moment.

Just how do you account for this range of abstract concepts with which the mind is at home? The Christian believes that, being created in the image of God, humans have the capacity for creativity, a potential even for nobility. But they are also fallen, and this explains their tendency to miss the mark and behave shabbily or much worse. There will be a tension between two natures – old Bibles call it 'the flesh' and 'the spirit' – but there is also hope, since an aspect of a Christian's redemption is a restoration, even in this life, of that divine spark within. Walking in the power of the Holy Spirit a believer may even demonstrate some of the Spirit's fruit: love, joy, peace, patience, kindness, goodness, faithfulness, gentleness and self-control. These are emotions which are not only understandable but, by the grace of God, even achievable.

Newman on mind

Nearly 170 years before the University of Oxford appointed you the first Charles Simonyi Professor of the Public Understanding of Science, a graduate of Trinity and Fellow of Oriel became vicar of St Mary's, the university church. During the last years of John Henry Newman's incumbency, it is said that there was scarcely a person of note in the university, old or young, who did not regularly attend the services and listen to his sermons. 'Who,' Matthew Arnold recalled forty years later, 'could resist the charm of that spiritual apparition, gliding in the dim afternoon light of the aisles of St Mary's, rising into the pulpit, and then, in the most entrancing of voices breaking the silence with words and thoughts which were a religious movement, subtle, sweet, mournful?'[114]

Seven years before Darwin completed his *Origin*, Newman wrote with his usual insight and eloquence about the power and uniqueness of the human mind. He thought that one of the first things the human mind does is to take hold of and appropriate what meets the senses. He believed that this was the main distinction between use of the senses by humans and animals. Animals gaze on sights and are arrested by sounds. What they see and hear are mainly sights and sounds only. The human intellect, on the other hand, energizes ear or eye as well and perceives in sights and sounds something beyond them. It seizes and unites what the senses present to it; it grasps and forms what need not have been seen or heard except in its constituent parts.

In the *Idea of a University* Newman wrote that the human mind:

> discerns in lines and colours, or in tones, what is beautiful and what is not. It gives them a meaning, and invests them with an idea. It gathers up a succession of notes into the expression of a whole, and calls it a melody; it has a keen sensibility towards angles and curves, lights and shadows, tints and contours. It distinguishes between rule and exception, between accident and design. It assigns phenomena to a general law, qualities to a subject, acts to a principle, and effects to a cause. In a word, it philosophizes; for I suppose science and philosophy, in their elementary

idea, are nothing else but this habit of *viewing*, as it may be called, the objects which sense conveys to the mind, of throwing them into system, and uniting and stamping them with form.[115]

Mind at home with abstract concepts

I think we can go further even further than Newman in saying that the mind is at home with these concepts. I would say that the mind *delights* in such abstract concepts. And each of these words individually opens up a rich area for thought and reflection. Abstraction is a wonderful property of the human mind, which has also given rise to language and indeed science. But the mind is also of course able to apply itself to the particular and the concrete.

A few years ago I cut a photograph from the London *Times*. It was of an Albanian grandmother who had been forced to escape to Macedonia from Kosovo by Serb forces who had handcuffed and taken away the young men of her village. I kept the photograph because of the depth of expression on the face of the old woman. There is more going on behind the lines of that face than can I think be accounted for by cumulative natural selection working in isolation from a world which was created and is sustained by an all-knowing and all-powerful Creator.

At the end of 2002 the forensic artist Melissa Dring produced a new portrait of Jane Austen based on contemporary evidence which provoked lively and generally admiring comment: 'this seems to sit well with a mental picture I have of her'; it 'captures that glance of humour and intelligence'; an 'appearance expressive of health and animation'.[116] Have you never noticed an expression flash across a friend's face that suggests to you a depth of reality and meaning that is beyond ourselves?

The conscience

As soon as people began to reflect on deep issues, and to record their conclusions, they believed there was something mysterious about the conscience. Socrates, for example, believed that he had a divine voice within him. He valued his conscience because it seemed somehow to be telling him how he ought to behave. None of us feels quite happy when we act against our 'better judgement'. Most of us know what it is like to toss and turn in bed, unable to sleep, when we know that one part of us has acted in a way of which another part disapproves.

Christians believe that conscience is unique to humans and that its effectiveness is increased by experience and the grace of God. A good conscience is a quiet conscience. Some of the early Christian Fathers spoke, like Socrates, of conscience as the voice of God within. Bishop Joseph Butler (1692–1752) thought of the conscience as a sort of moral sense, through which, when we exercise it, we become aware of the presence of God. John Wesley thought of conscience as the 'internal witness' of the Holy Spirit. Immanuel Kant thought of conscience as the awareness of the universal claim of the moral dictates of reason (his 'Categorical Imperative'). Religion recognizes this claim as God's will, but since we are rational beings with free will we can act against our consciences – although curiously we feel uncomfortable when we do so.

I know that Freudian psychology challenges these views, regarding conscience as the activity of the super-ego which is formed in childhood and represses drives that are socially unacceptable. I am aware also that people produce examples that are alleged to prove that conscience appears to approve or disapprove of different types of behaviour according to geography and culture. That is why moral theologians stress the need for conscience to be informed by paying attention to the teaching of Scripture and the Church.

The idea of conscience, however, *makes sense* – so much so that the 'dictates of conscience' are enshrined in the United Nations' Universal Declaration of Human Rights and it is well understood in Parliament that on some issues MPs and Peers should be allowed to vote according to their consciences. I think that your atheistic worldview, which depends so heavily on natural selection for its understanding of our responses to reality, has great difficulty in accounting for the curious but recognizable phenomenon of conscience.

7

Consciousness

Earlier in this letter, I described how Wallace grappled with the problem of consciousness: that mysterious characteristic of humankind by which we are aware of ourselves. I warm to your honesty on this subject. I noticed that at the debate in 1999 arranged by the *Guardian* 'Is science killing the soul?' when Steven Pinker of the Massachusetts Institute of Technology was assuring us that an exhaustive computational approach to neuroscience and psychology will eventually eliminate the difficulty posed by the question of consciousness, you intervened to say: 'It still feels like a hell of a problem for me' – and you have consistently admitted this in your books, despite the grand assertion in your famous sentence about a mystery which has been solved.

You have frankly called consciousness 'the most profound mystery facing modern biology'[117] and at one point in *The Selfish Gene* you say that you are not philosopher enough to discuss it. At another place in the same book you describe consciousness as 'the culmination of an evolutionary trend towards the emancipation of survival machines as executive decision-takers from their ultimate masters, the genes'.[118] You suggest that our brains are in charge of the day-to-day running of survival-machine affairs. They have the power to rebel against the genes, for example by deciding to use contraceptives to avoid having as many children as the body they control might be able. Genes are the policy-makers; brains are the executives.

Steve Rose insists that your argument here is unsatisfactory. He says that either we are the products of our genes, or we aren't. If we are, it must be that our genes are not merely selfish but also rebellious, building the structures that give our brains the power to contradict our bodies. But in that case, why is it that the brains of our near evolutionary neighbours – say, chimps – are not as rebellious as ours?[119]

Somehow humans have come to have brains immeasurably more powerful and adaptable than the cleverest computer we have ever built – indeed, more complex than stars, which by comparison turn out to be quite simple. Our possession of both brains and consciousness is a mystery that requires explanation at a number of different levels to do it full justice. How does a purely physical mechanism like the brain produce phenomena like thoughts, feelings, dreams, images and intentions?

The uniqueness of human consciousness

Roger Penrose has reflected deeply on consciousness. He notes that many people think it will soon be possible to build computers capable of artificial intelligence (AI) – machines that could equal or beat the thought processes of the human mind. Penrose does not agree. He thinks that what goes on in the mind is very different from the workings of any computer.

Penrose thinks of humans as unique, mysterious, almost miraculous beings. In *The Emperor's New Mind* he expresses his scepticism towards the notion that the brain is a digital computer. His argument is that the simulation in a computer of anything that could pass for genuine intelligence has not been achieved; there are no computers that possess 'understanding'.

Many supporters of AI think our present conscious perceptions are merely the enacting of algorithms. An algorithm is a calculational procedure of some kind, such as that used in a thermostat to keep water at a constant temperature. Penrose argues that there is surely more to our feelings of awareness than mere algorithms. Inside our heads, there is a magnificent structure that controls our actions and somehow evokes an awareness of the world around us. How does the brain achieve the miracles that we know it to be capable of? Although much has been written about the brain, that is still a difficult question to answer – especially for those who rule out the idea that we are made in the image of a Creator with mind.

Penrose thinks that neither classical nor quantum mechanics will ever explain the way we think. He thinks there must be a non-algorithmic ingredient to thought processes. He points out that conscious reflection can sometimes enable him to arrive at the truth of a mathematical statement in a way that no algorithm could. He argues that algorithms in themselves never ascertain truth. You could as easily make an algorithm produce nothing but lies as you could make it produce truths. You need external insights in order to decide the validity of an algorithm. He thinks that this ability to distinguish truth from falsehood is one of the distinctive features of consciousness.[120]

Notwithstanding your view that life is nothing more than bytes of digital information, and in that sense comparable to a computer, most people would doubt that a mere computer could ever feel pleasure or pain, enjoy poetry or the beauty of an evening sky or the magic of sounds. A computer cannot hope or love or despair, or have a genuine purpose in life.

When we talk of consciousness, there will always be something essential that is missing from computers. It is consciousness that makes us aware of the very existence of the universe. It is remarkable that the organization of matter has reached the stage where it has attained knowledge of both itself and the universe. And many people also report that their consciousness is aware of something beyond themselves which they call God and who corresponds in their minds to the Creator of both the universe and themselves.

The debate

In his introduction to the *Guardian* debate, Tim Radford asked: 'What is this mind for? Why is it so big? Why does any mind seem to be able to encompass absolutely everything? It's all we've got, but we're not that conscious of it. We think we're occupying reality, but of course it's only our brain that tells us this.'

I have already noted that, when you spoke as one of the invited guests, you honestly admitted that you did not understand consciousness and that you do not think any other scientist does either. You went on to criticize what you termed the 'dishonest trick' of using words like soul or spirit as if they constituted an explanation.

But the Bible does not offer the spiritual dimension as an explanation for anything. On the contrary, from the moment of its introductory assertion 'In the beginning God . . .' it continues, on the whole, to assume the existence of God, only rarely considering the possibility of atheism as at Psalm 14:1: 'The fool says in his heart, "There is no God."'

Steven Pinker seemed more confident that science was moving towards some sort of understanding of consciousness. In proposing the idea that the mind is the physiological activity of the brain, in particular the information processing activity of the brain, he put himself at odds both with Roger Penrose and Susan Greenfield (whom I quote below). Pinker stresses that the brain, like other organs, is shaped by the genes; and that in turn, the genome was shaped by natural selection and, what he calls, 'other evolutionary processes'. This is not a shocking claim to him. Rather, he believes that there is great excitement in fleshing out the details and showing exactly how our perception, decision-making and emotions can be tied to the activity of the brain. He thinks that we are learning more and more every day about the neural basis of consciousness. The part that remains a mystery for him is why the 'purely subjective aspect of experience' (to use his phrase) should exist at all and he thinks it's possible that the existence of subjective first-person experience is not explainable by science.

Brain, mind, self and consciousness

Professor Susan Greenfield, a neuroscientist, is much closer to Penrose than to Pinker. Her argument in *The Private Life of the Brain* (2001) brings no comfort to anyone who wants to make a simple equation between brain and mind or who is a strong believer in the idea of artificial intelligence. One of her main conclusions is close, if not identical, to a key insight articulated by the founder of Christianity.

She begins by reminding us that there are 100 billion brain cells, or *neurons*, in the adult human brain. As the brain becomes more sophisticated, it appears to exploit instinct less and instead uses increasingly the results of individual experience, of learning. We are born with most of the neurons we are ever going to have, so something else must go on within our postnatal skulls. It is not the brain cells themselves that change and continue to change, so much as the *connections* between them. The neurons do not increase in number, but the connections between them become increasingly conspicuous, pushing the main bodies of the neurons ever farther apart, as though they were clasping hands with one another and then unfolding and stretching out their tiny arms. Only once these connections are in place, networking one brain cell with another, are neurons able to communicate with one another. Only then will the brain be able to work to its full potential and start to interpret the world in the light of experience.

As this process continues, individuality becomes more evident: the balance starts to tip away from nature toward nurture – the effects of our surroundings and experiences. This personalization of the brain, crafted over the long years of childhood and continuing to develop throughout life, creates that unique pattern of connections between brain cells which she thinks of as 'mind'.

The mind, Professor Greenfield says, is something more than a lump of gray matter. She insists that the functions of the brain cannot be compartmentalized in a mechanistic way and thinks of mind as the seething morass of cell circuitry which is not given but has been configured by personal experience and is constantly being updated as we live out each moment. Important factors in making us the persons we are are the personal experiences we alone have had, what amounts to our own memories. The personalization of the physical brain is driven not so much by genes as by individual experiences. Thus the concepts of *memories, mind* and *self* are closely related.

The building blocks of consciousness

When people are 'out of their minds' with fear or ecstasy, they are no longer accessing that highly personalized set of values, history and unique view of life. They are no longer making full use of their personalized configurations of brain connections, which Professor Greenfield defines as the mind. Emotions are the building blocks of consciousness. Emotions are with us all the time, to a greater or lesser degree, depending on how much we are using, or losing, our minds at any one moment. One cannot understand consciousness without understanding emotion. Consciousness is not purely rational or cognitive as those working in artificial, computational systems have implied.

Emotion is the most basic form of consciousness. Minds develop as brains do, both as a species and as an individual starts to escape genetic programming in favour of personal, experienced-based learning. The more you have of emotion at any particular moment, then the less you have of mind and vice versa.

When we fall asleep and lose consciousness, we do not expect to lose our minds as well. Our brains are there when we sleep, waiting to be accessed next morning. So, in addition to the bundle of memories, however they are realized in the brain, some special, additional process is at work amid the 'bump and grind' of our otherwise automated grey matter.

Not comparable to computers or AI

Professor Greenfield's conclusions are similar to Penrose's, though she writes after more than a decade of further research. Consider sophisticated robots crawling around and bumping into the equivalents of coffee tables or TV sets as they learn to navigate their little worlds, literally, by trial and error. This model may suggest that the biological brain might work like a computer. But it would be the same type of mind that you and I have when we are fast asleep. Susan Greenfield maintains that even the most sophisticated robots do not have a brain, or more accurately an inner life, that is in any way comparable with that of its conscious biological counterpart. No robot is anywhere near becoming *aware*. Since most AI models focus exclusively on experience-driven adaptive processes, it is no surprise that they tell us little about consciousness and emotions.

Like Roger Penrose, Susan Greenfield finds it hard to see how AI models will ever acquire the most exciting aspects of brain function, understanding and indeed consciousness. *Pace* Steven Pinker she is astonished at how consciousness manages to produce that unified state we experience most of the time. Over our lifetimes we generate intellectual inner resources. The mind is a long-term, lifelong, personalized brain.

Pinker defines *mind* as 'what the brain does'. He thinks of the brain as a very good computational device and combines this with an ultra-evolutionary approach, inspired by the theory of natural selection, combined with the basic concept of genes unswervingly bent on replication. Professor Greenfield responds that this computational model is limited to learning and memory skills that can be measured objectively, and which can be performed easily by a machine. Unfortunately, the approach is of no help at all in understanding the more slippery phenomena that so far seem to be unique to biological brains. Pinker assures us that an exhaustive computational approach to neuroscience and psychology will eventually eliminate the difficulty posed by the question of consciousness. 'And yet,' says Greenfield, 'we are still left in the dark as to how we would ever compute a headache or the exhilaration of first love. The computational approach cannot really help with the issue of emotion and the related question of consciousness itself.'[121]

Susan Greenfield is left wondering how the subjective feeling of emotions such as pleasure actually evolved –

and why. Nothing else has come along like the biological brain in the universe. It would therefore be surprising if it could be modelled in terms of other things and yet retain the most exciting and as yet unidentified properties that produce a state of self-awareness.

Despite the explosion of ideas about consciousness and the mind that have been presented over the last decade or so, Professor Greenfield thinks that there has been little real progress. 'We need to know what is happening in the real brain and yet the big question that scientists are still ducking is how the actual feel of emotions, raw consciousness no less, is accommodated in the physical mass.' How do we access the information in the brain? How does the brain's 'index' work?[122]

All our physical brains look pretty much the same, but our minds are quintessentially our own. As we live, memories pile up, and this accumulation of past scenarios, all stored within our brains, gives us a unique perspective from which to interpret the flood of sensations that bombard us every waking moment. Memories and mind are inextricably linked.

Denial of Self

The mind grows slowly as a life story takes shape and persists throughout nightly ruptures in awareness. As we develop, the contribution of the mind will be to enhance each conscious moment by imputing each snapshot of the outside world with meaning. Life starts like a lens out of focus with blurred and abstract shapes, but the growth of a mind enables us to home in with increasing precision on specific objects and people.

The essence of pleasure, says Susan Greenfield, is denial – she uses the word 'abrogation' – of the Self. Emotions – especially when their expression is accompanied by a loss of self-control – can sweep away all sense of self. The more the mind predominates over raw emotion, the deeper the consciousness. A deeper consciousness is a world laden with personal meaning.

She has come to adopt the basic idea that emotions are a denial of the Self. She finds it impossible to distinguish *mind* from the concept of *Self*. 'After all, if *mind* is the personalization of the brain, then what more, or what less, could *Self* actually be?'[123] She thinks the two terms might as well be synonymous. For virtually all animals except humans, and especially for infant humans, the under-developed mind would entail a lack of self-consciousness. Consciousness will blossom into self-consciousness only when enough associations are in place to be able to provide a common reference point to myriad experiences, like a hub on a wheel.

Emotions often, but not always, involve relinquishing inner control. When the Apostle Paul lists a cluster of qualities which he terms 'the fruit of the Spirit' (Galatians 5:22) several of them could be called emotions, such as love and joy, but the list includes self-control. Our inner self-life is changing all the time. Even within a day, within an hour, we are different. All the time experiences leave their mark and in turn determine how we interpret new experiences. As the mind develops, as we 'understand' everything more deeply, we have increasing control over what happens to us: we are self-conscious. But this self-consciousness itself is not fixed: it will ebb and flow in inverse relation to emotions from one moment to the next. We cannot expect to be in a state of simple pleasure all the time. Such, according to Susan Greenfield, is the paradox of our adult human existence.

The paradox of the Self

Jesus memorably expressed the same insight about self-denial two thousand years before Susan Greenfield first entered the Laboratory of Pharmacology in Oxford. He spoke with both simplicity and profundity when he said: 'If anyone would come after me, he must deny himself and take up his cross and follow me. For whoever wants to save his life will lose it, but whoever loses his life for me will find it. What good will it be for a man if he gains the whole world, yet forfeits his soul? Or what can a man give in exchange for his soul?' (Matthew 16:24–26).

At the heart of Christianity is the same paradox that Greenfield identifies in her studies of the working of the brain and its link with mind and consciousness: we find ourselves by losing ourselves; we discover our true selves by giving ourselves away in self-denial. This paradox lying at the heart of the Christian faith may be a clue to the nature of ultimate reality.

The German pastor Dietrich Bonhoeffer wrote strikingly that, 'When Christ calls a man, he bids him come and die.'[124] The central emblem of the Christian faith, the cross, speaks not only of something Christ has done for us: it is also a symbol of death to self. But alongside the Lord's call to self-denial is his assurance about self-affirmation (if you lose your life you find it). He spoke of the value of human beings in God's sight. They are much more valuable than birds and animals. I know you condemn this idea as 'speciesist' but Jesus does seem to have held to the idea that human beings *are* the crown of God's creative activity and that he made male and female in his own image. It is the divine image we bear which gives us our distinctive value. As one young American black, rebelling against inferiority feelings inculcated in him by whites, is reported to have inscribed on a banner in his room: 'I'm me and I'm good, 'cause God don't make junk.'

But how can we value ourselves and deny ourselves simultaneously? The answer is that our 'Self' is a complex mixture of good and evil, glory and shame. The Self we are to deny, disown and crucify is what Christians think of as the fallen self, everything in us which is incompatible with Jesus (hence his command to deny *yourself* and then follow *him*). The Self we are to affirm and value is our created self, everything within us which is compatible with Jesus (hence his assurance that if we lose ourselves by self-denial we shall find ourselves). True self-denial (the denial of our false fallen self) is the road to self-discovery not self-destruction.

Whatever we are by creation, we affirm: our rationality and sense of moral obligation. What we are by the Fall, we deny or repudiate: our irrationality and moral perversity. Susan Greenfield arrived at the same insight by a different but no less valuable route.

The idea of divine experience

During the *Guardian* debate, Tim Radford asked a question: 'If there is a sense of good which is independent of us, who put it there? If a sense of god is a product of evolution, why do we all have such a consistent idea of a divine experience? When one reads the lives of the saints, one comes across the same phenomenon. We don't all have the same brains, but why do we have a similar conception of what it means to be spiritual?'

It was a good question – but, sadly, neither Steven Pinker nor you answered it. You actually steered the question in another direction. You asked Steven whether the feeling you have that you are a single entity, who makes decisions, and loves and hates and has political views and so on, is a kind of illusion that has come about because Darwinian selection found it expedient to create that illusion of unitariness rather than let us be a kind of society of mind.

Steven Pinker may have thought this a far-fetched suggestion of yours, but, whatever the reason, he did not give you an answer. But if you read Susan Greenfield's books you will find that she speaks of this sense of harmony of thought and identity that we all experience as one of the mysteries of consciousness.

8

God and the Universe

You told the American organization *Counterbalance* that you cannot understand why so many people who are sophisticated in science go on believing in God. You think that in some cases what they mean by God is very different from what ordinary people mean by God. 'There are physicists who are deeply awed, as I am,' you said, 'by the majesty of the universe, by the mystery of origins – the origins of the laws of physics, the fundamental constants of physics – and who are moved by this to say there is something so mysterious that it is almost like God, and maybe use the metaphor of God. God is in the equations. God is in the fundamental constants. And that's fine. I mean, that's just redefinition of that which we find mysterious at the basis of the universe.'

I agree with you that some physicists appear to use the word 'God' in this way. But I know other physicists who not only believe that God is in the equations and the constants but who also identify that mystery with their orthodox Christian understanding of God. Before I consider further what that idea is, I observe that you acknowledge (despite the sweeping claims of your famous sentence) that there is in fact mystery in the universe.

Mysterious, but orderly

In your Dimbleby lecture you pointed out, quite rightly, that the universe, though mysterious, is orderly:

> There is mystery in the universe, beguiling mystery, but it isn't capricious, whimsical, frivolous in its changeability. The universe is an orderly place and, at a deep level, regions of it behave like other regions, times behave like other times. If you put a brick on a table it stays there unless something lawfully moves it, even if you meanwhile forget it's there. Poltergeists and sprites don't intervene and hurl it about for reasons of mischief or caprice. There is mystery, but not magic, strangeness beyond the wildest imagining, but no spells or witchery, no arbitrary miracles.

Alfred Wallace was also impressed by the uniformity of matter and of physical and chemical laws throughout our universe. If he had lived another fourteen years to read the big bang theory, he would have been intrigued to reflect that after the bang the expansion of the universe was in a precisely ordered way, in accordance with a set of basic mathematical constants and laws which have governed its subsequent development.

In addition to the four fundamental forces of 'nature' (gravity, strong nuclear, weak interaction and electro-magnetic), we can say that all the incredibly diverse phenomena we see in nature are characterized by just a small number of laws, each of which can be written in a simple and elegant mathematical form.

There are:

- laws of mechanics which can be expressed as Hamilton's Equations
- laws of electrodynamics which can be expressed as Maxwell's Equations

- laws of statistical mechanics which can be expressed as Boltzmann's Equations
- laws of quantum mechanics which can be expressed as Schrodinger's Equations
- laws of General Relativity which can be expressed as Einstein's Equation.

And then there are universal constants such as Planck's constant, the speed of light, the masses of the proton and electron, the unit charge for the electron or proton, the electromagnetic coupling constants, Boltzmann's constant and so on.

Why is it that the nature and behaviour of the universe can be captured by a relatively small number of pure, often elegant, mathematical formulae? Is it not surprising that this should be so? Believers in God naturally think that all this comprehensibility has its origin in a cosmic mind. Stephen Hawking has observed that, 'It would be completely consistent with all we know to say that there was a Being who is responsible for the laws of physics.'[125]

These basic laws are such as to produce atoms capable of combining into molecules and assembling themselves into the complicated strings needed to produce life forms. Where did these laws come from? How did they come to take the forms they did take? And how did they come to interrelate with one another so as to make possible a coherent universe?

It is striking that a law, like Newton's law of gravity, is (as far as we can tell) a universal truth. So is the second law of thermodynamics. The orbits of the planets around the sun are predictable and we can safely assume that apples are not going suddenly to start falling upwards out of trees.

Even the claim that a physicist or mathematician will one day discover a grand Theory of Everything is really an admission that this universe is magnificently if strangely coherent.

Since you reject the idea of a Creator, it is surely an extra-ordinary coincidence that there exists any matter or energy which is governed by the laws of physics. There might have been no universe, no matter, no laws of physics. Or there might have been something to which laws did not apply, or the laws might have ceased to exist soon after coming into being. That is, events might not have continued behaving in the regular predictable ways that can be described by the laws of nature. The fact that there are laws which continue to operate on matter and energy in predictable ways is a surprising fact, which might well have been otherwise.

A universe in which the laws of physics were as ephemeral as the tastes of fashion would be a nightmare. We all rely on the stability of the universe. The law of gravity is the same on earth as it is on the moon. To be strictly accurate, we should say that if the laws are changing, they are changing very slowly indeed. But for all practical purposes, they remain the same.

The Anthropic Principle

Roughly speaking the anthropic principle says that we see the universe the way it is, at least in part, because we exist. There are a number of different versions of the principle and these range, as Stephen Hawking puts it, 'from those that are so weak as to be trivial to those that are so strong as to be absurd'.[126]

The idea was introduced in an influential book of the same name by physicists John Barrow and Frank Tipler.[127] The essence of the idea lies in the fact that when physicists look at the basic physical laws of nature, and at the basic physical constants, what they find is that many of these laws and constants seem to be remarkably finely balanced in such a way as to make life possible. One simple example of this is the laws of gravity and electromagnetism.

The gravitational and electric forces obey 'inverse square laws' – in other words, the force of attraction or repulsion between two bodies falls off by the reciprocal of the square of the distance between them.

If the force–distance relationship were anything other than an inverse square law then solar systems and atoms would not be stable. If the gravitational force were any stronger, stable solar systems could not form because planets would quickly spiral into the sun. In the same way, if the electric force were any stronger, stable atoms would not be able to form because electrons would spiral into the nucleus. And if the gravitational force were any weaker, planets would tend to drift off into space and not remain in orbit. So it seems that the inverse square law is particularly convenient. It not only allows the formation of atoms (which are essential for the evolution of life), it also allows the formation of solar systems to provide nice safe homes for you, me and all our friends.

I read that the universe is full of examples like this, where the very nature of a physical law, or the very value of some crucial physical constant (such as the proton to electron mass ratio) seems to be 'just-so'. Any change in its value would seem to throw the structure or stability of the universe so out of kilter that it is hard to see how life could ever evolve in such a universe. To physicists such as Barrow and Tipler this implies that something has carefully 'tuned' the laws of nature so that life would evolve. To these scientists, the very laws of nature suggest the presence at least of Wallace's thoughtful intelligence acting behind the scenes – a mysterious being who in some sense wanted beings like you and me to evolve.

Although we should be cautious about making exaggerated claims for anthropic arguments, they do represent an embarrassment to atheism, which offers us no argument for why the universe should bother to exist. Denis Alexander writes:

Our finely tuned universe is not just any old 'something', but contains within it a planet full of people who postulate theories about cosmology and the meaning of the universe, who write poetry, fall in love, build socially complex societies, and who believe in justice, freedom, ethics and the reality of good and evil. Atheism provides no insights into why such an odd entity should exist, nor for why the physical parameters of the universe should be so precisely correct as to make such an entity possible ... The finely tuned physical and cosmological constants of the universe, together with the presence in the universe of conscious beings, are together clearly consistent with the notion of a personal God who has intentions for the universe that he had brought into being and continues to sustain.[128]

The Creator with a pin

In *The Emperor's New Mind* Roger Penrose asks us to picture the Creator, armed with a pin. He has to place the pin at some point in space/time. Each different positioning of the pin results in a different universe. The accuracy that is needed for the Creator's aim depends upon the entropy – the degree of disorder – of the universe that is thereby created. It would be easier to produce a high-entropy universe. But to start off the universe in a state of low entropy, and one where there will be a second law of thermodynamics, the Creator has to be much more precise in his aim. How tiny would the region be he has to aim for in order that a universe closely resembling the one in which we actually live would result?

Penrose calculated that the Creator's aim must have been to an accuracy of one part in 10 to the power of 10 to the power of 123! This, Penrose tells us, is an extraordinary figure. It would be impossible to write the number down in full in an ordinary system of notation: it would be one followed by 10 to the power of 123 successive noughts![129]

Einstein on coherence

Many reflective people have been impressed by the coherence and dependability of the universe. In 1936, Albert Einstein wrote to a friend,

> You may find it strange that I consider the comprehensibility of the world to the degree that we may speak of such comprehensibility as a miracle or an eternal mystery. Well, *a priori* one should expect a chaotic world, which cannot be in any way grasped through thought . . . The kind of order created, for example, by Newton's theory of gravity is of quite a different kind. Even if the axioms of the theory are posited by a human being, the success of such an enterprise presupposes an order in the objective world of a high degree, which one has no *a priori* right to expect. This is the miracle which grows increasingly persuasive with the increasing development of knowledge.[130]

Two years later, Einstein wrote: 'Without the belief that it is possible to grasp the reality with our theoretical constructions, without the belief in the inner harmony of our world, there could be no science. This belief is and always will remain the fundamental motive for all scientific creation.' Einstein stood in a long tradition of scientists who were convinced of the existence of some basic order.

The mysterious usefulness of mathematics

The physicist, Eugene Wigner, wrote in 1960 that, 'the enormous usefulness of mathematics is something bordering on the mysterious . . . There is no rational explanation for it . . . The miracle of the appropriateness of the language of mathematics for the formulation of the laws of physics is a wonderful gift that we neither understand nor deserve.'[131]

More recently, the physicist Paul Davies has said, 'the equations of physics have in them incredible simplicity, elegance and beauty. That in itself is sufficient to prove to me that there must be a God who is responsible for these laws and responsible for the universe.'[132]

According to the Christian's worldview, the comprehensibility and mathematical elegance of the universe and the presence of conscious persons in our world is both coherent and expected. Are not these phenomena anomalies for those who follow your atheistic worldview?

Did the universe know we were coming?

In a frequently quoted passage, Freeman Dyson, a now-retired physicist from Princeton's Institute for Advanced Study, has written, 'As we look into the universe and identify the many accidents of physics and astronomy that have worked to our benefit, it almost seems as if the universe must in some sense have known that we were coming.'[133]

And Arno Penzias wrote, 'Astronomy leads us to a unique event, a universe which was created out of nothing and delicately balanced to provide exactly the right conditions required to support life. In the absence of an absurdly-improbable accident, the observations of modern science seem to suggest an underlying, one might say, supernatural plan.'[134]

Sir Fred Hoyle, the British astronomer and mathematician, believed in the early 1950s that the coincidences in the universe which allowed the origin and development of life were just that – coincidences. But in the 1980s, he wrote: 'Such properties seem to run through the fabric of the natural world like a thread of happy coincidences. But there are so many odd coincidences essential to life that some explanation seems required to account for them.'[135]

If life follows from matter with causal dependability, perhaps God has told the laws of nature to 'Make life!' And, through life, its by-products: mind, knowledge and understanding. It means that the laws of the universe have ensured their own comprehension.

What sort of a universe is it in which chemicals in a primeval soup have organized themselves into objects like us who are not only conscious but *self*-conscious? We can reflect, and love and hate, and pray, have ideas, write long letters to Oxford professors, exhibit the creative genius of Mozart or Shakespeare, or display the personal qualities of Mother Teresa or Jesus. What sort of a universe do we live in?

9

God and Baseball Hats

You coined the word 'meme' to describe cultural entities which replicate in rather the same way that DNA does. You quote the habit of wearing a baseball hat backwards as something that has spread around the western world like an epidemic. In *The Selfish Gene* you go on to say that: 'The survival of the god meme in the meme pool results from its great psychological appeal. It provides a superficially plausible answer to deep and troubling questions about existence. It suggests that injustices in this world may be rectified in the next. The "everlasting arms" hold out a cushion against our own inadequacies which, like a doctor's placebo, is none the less effective for being imaginary.'[136]

Denis Alexander has pointed out how inaccurate your analogy of the meme is:

[I]t is simply not the case that ideas or beliefs are transmitted in a way similar to genes. Genes are transmitted as DNA sequences incorporated into chromosomes. The communica-tion of ideas and beliefs is made by verbal, pictorial or written communication and is nothing like DNA replication . . . many of our beliefs are absorbed with little thought through our early upbringing, but equally we can assess our beliefs in later life, think rationally about them and change them if we wish to do so. This is quite dissimilar from our genetic inheritance, about which we can do relatively little.[137]

And your reference to the 'everlasting arms' acting as a cushion ties in with your expressed belief that people may become religious for reasons of 'personal comfort'. But you should note that following Christ is highly demanding. It might involve, as it has for some, giving up a lucrative job to serve God and neighbour in a socially deprived area. For some, Christ's call to 'carry the cross' has involved the ultimate sacrifice of martyrdom. Perhaps that is why Jesus observed that 'small is the gate and narrow the road that leads to life, and only a few find it' (Matthew 7:14).

Religion and education

In the interview with Madeleine Pym of the British Humanist Association published in September 2002, you asserted that:

> Religion teaches you to be satisfied with non-explanations for things as though they were explanations and, in some cases even, that belief without evidence is a positive virtue. It stifles the sort of investigative approach to the world which I think is an unequivocally good thing and which has led to most of the progress which humanity has made. I think that religion is actively subversive of genuine education, that it actually is inimical to true education.

Of course there is some truth in this in the sense that it would not be too difficult to find examples that fitted your description either in the contemporary world or in church history, but as a generalization it is monstrously unfair. In the eleventh century, Archbishop Anselm of Canterbury expressed the formula *fides quaerens intellectum* ('faith seeking understanding'), a formula that became a rallying cry for Christians who pursued serious scholarship. Because people have been endowed with reason, they have an urge to express their experience of faith intellectually, to translate the contents of faith into concepts, and to formulate beliefs in a systematic understanding of the correlation between God, humankind and creation. Justin Martyr, a professional philosopher, saw Christian revelation as the fulfillment, not the elimination, of philosophical understanding.

In the medieval western world, theology became the instructor of the different subject areas – grammar, rhetoric, dialectic, music, arithmetic, geometry and astronomy – which were incorporated into the system of education as 'servants of theology'. This approach to education became part of the structure of the universities that were founded in the thirteenth century. The different sciences only gradually gained a certain independence.

With the Reformation there was widespread concern for education as a result of the Reformers' stress on the importance of the Scriptures being made available to everyone. Their concern was the beginning of universal, public education. Luther also argued that it was necessary for society that its youth be educated. He held that it was the duty of civil authorities to compel their subjects to keep their children in school so 'that there will always be preachers, jurists, pastors, writers, physicians, schoolmasters, and the like, for we cannot do without them.'[138]

Open conflict between science and theology occurred only when the traditional biblical view of the world was seriously questioned, as in the case of the Italian astronomer Galileo (1633). However, the principles of Galileo's scientific research were themselves the result of a Christian idea of science and truth – and Galileo retained his Christian faith and commitment despite his brushes with the Church. The biblical faith in God as Creator and incarnate Redeemer is an explicit affirmation of the goodness, reality, and dependence of the created world on the Creator – assumptions underlying scientific work through most of its history in the western world.

Virtually the whole of the British education down to village level emerged from a church-based, sponsored system and a western-style, liberal education was made available to many countries of the world by courtesy of Christian missions.

In the twentieth century, William Temple asserted that Christianity was an avowedly materialistic religion (God creates the material world and sees that it is good). Indeed, a positive relationship between education and science has been dominant in the history of Christianity, even though the opposite attitude has arisen occasionally during certain periods. Kepler spoke of celebrating God in science and, already in this letter, I have referred to prominent scientists throughout history who have been believers.

In 1997 the results of a survey conducted by two historians, Edward Larson and Larry Witham, were published. They had sent a questionnaire to one thousand randomly picked names from the then current edition of *American Men and Women of Science*. Of those who responded, 39.3 per cent declared themselves to be believers in a personal God who answers prayer, 46.3 per cent expressed disbelief, while 14.5 per cent remained agnostic. The results were much the same as in a similar survey which had been conducted in 1916, suggesting that nearly a century of scientific and technological advance had had little effect on the personal religious belief among American scientists.[139]

Your objections to God

When Sheena McDonald interviewed you on Channel 4, you told her that a Creator who created the universe or set up the laws of physics so that life would evolve or who actually supervised the evolution of life, would have to be some sort of super-intelligence, some sort of mega-mind.

> That mega-mind would have had to be present right at the start of the universe. The whole message of evolution is that complexity and intelligence and all the things that would go with being a creative force come late, they come as a consequence of hundreds of millions of years of natural selection. There was no intelligence early on in the universe. Intelligence arose, it's arisen here, maybe it's arisen on lots of other places in the universe. Maybe somewhere in some other galaxy there is a super-intelligence so colossal that from our point of view it would be a god. But it cannot have been the sort of God that we need to explain the origin of the universe, because it cannot have been there that early.

You agreed with Sheena when she intervened at this point to check that you were saying that religion is peddling a fundamental untruth. 'Science offers us an explanation of how complexity (the difficult) arose out of simplicity (the easy),' you continued. 'The hypothesis of God offers no worthwhile explanation for anything, for it simply postulates what we are trying to explain. It postulates the difficult to explain, and leaves it at that. We cannot prove that there is no God, but we can safely conclude that He is very, very improbable indeed.'[140]

Religion 'peddling an untruth'

This 'untruth' you say religion is peddling has fooled a lot of people including, in the case of Christianity, some pretty able minds. If we draw up a list of some of the classic Christian thinkers we remember that the earliest of them lived just a few generations after the founder of Christianity himself: I think of Ignatius, Tertullian,

Chrysostom, Augustine, Benedict, Anselm, Bernard of Clairvaux, Francis of Assisi, Thomas Aquinas, Julian of Norwich, Catherine of Siena, Thomas à Kempis, Erasmus, Thomas More, Luther, Calvin, George Herbert, Pascal, Bunyan, Wesley, Kierkegaard, Tolstoy, Spurgeon, C.S. Lewis, Bonhoeffer, William Temple, Michael Ramsey and Solzhenitsyn. Or we think of Christian poets down through the centuries like Caedmon, Donne, Milton, Watts, Cowper, Blake, Keble, Newman, Rossetti, Manley Hopkins, Coleridge, T.S. Eliot, W.H. Auden – all, according to you, peddling an untruth, spreading a virus.

Or reflect on Christian art down through the centuries: the simple drawings on the walls of the catacombs under the streets of Rome; the icons of the Orthdox church; Giotto's frescos in the hilltop churches of north Italy; Botticelli's *Mystic Nativity*; Rembrandt's *Shepherds Worshipping the Child*; the stained glass windows in Chartres Cathedral; Della Robbia's sensitive face of Jesus; mosaics of Christ in majesty in a Byzantine church; or I think of the tail plate of a taxi in Haiti showing a colourful West Indian rendering of Jesus riding into Jerusalem on a donkey. Is all this glorious art based on a lie and inspired by nothing?

Morality

You have said that Jesus' command to love our neighbour is good and you would not wish to downplay it. You think we benefit from social institutions that encourage us towards moral behaviour. You believe it important to have law and to have a moral education. You think we should try to inculcate into children moral rules, such as 'Do as you would be done by.' You agree that it is important to do moral philosophy, to try to work out the principles we want to live by rather than following biological dictates.

But you see no reason why these principles should be religious.

In the interview with the British Humanist Association (BHA) you considered the issue of whether some social force has been at work homogenizing the moral views of particular societies. You concluded that religion could not be such a force, since if it were we would expect to find some strong correlation between that moral consensus and, for example, what is written down in holy books. You argued that we do not find such a consensus and added that 'if you take the holy books literally we should all be stoning adulterers to death and that kind of thing, but we don't'.

I hope you are aware of the distinction which is often made between 'religion' and 'following Christ'. On one occasion, Jesus came face to face with a group who argued that if they took their holy book literally they should stone to death a woman who had been found out as an adulterer and now stood before them and him. I'm sure you recall his wise suggestion that 'If any one of you is without sin, let him be the first to throw a stone at her' (John 8:7) – the sort of observation made in a difficult situation which has helped to ensure his place in history for two thousand years.

You went on to tell the BHA that you did not have a fully framed answer to what makes our morality but that you were pretty sure it was not religion. 'I would like to see,' you went on, 'unequivocally, a decline in the influence of religion. I think it is a great evil. I think it makes for an enormous amount of unhappiness, and the world would unquestionably be a better place without it.'

I suppose this sense of morality arrived in your mind as a 'meme'. But I think that with your atheistic worldview you have a problem in resolving moral issues – even in defining words like 'evil' in the first place. And indeed you told Nick Pollard that you would be 'quite open to persuasion that killing people is right in some circum-stances'.[141]

In refusing to allow religion a role in establishing moral principles, you part company with Darwin, who wrote in *The Descent of Man*: 'With the more civilized races, the conviction of the existence of an all-seeing Deity has had a potent influence on the advance of morality.'[142] I have already noted Darwin's loyal support of the South American Missionary Society.

You admitted that you find it difficult to say where you get your 'ought' statements from. You do not feel as strongly about them as 'is' statements. If someone says that something is wrong, like killing people, you do not find that nearly such a defensible statement as 'I am a distant cousin of an orang-utan.' You can explain why the second of these statements is true. You are sure that it is true. But you do not believe the statement 'killing people is wrong' is of that character.

You told *Third Way* magazine that you feel unequipped to produce moral arguments in the way that you feel equipped to produce arguments of a cosmological and biological kind. I notice, however, that your feeling of inadequacy in producing moral arguments does not prevent you from making sweeping statements about religion.

They carved some of Kant's words on his gravestone in Königsberg: 'Two things fill my mind with ever-increasing wonder and awe, the more often and the more intensely the reflection dwells on them: the starry Heavens above me and the moral law within me.'

'Intrinsic value'; beauty

Evolution started hundreds of million years ago from a state in which there was just matter. No values were appreciated or understood and there was no consciousness.

Today the process of evolution has arrived at a state in which highly structured, self-replicating organisms know, feel and act. What is more, these organisms – people – are capable of producing and enjoying states of intrinsic value, desirable for their own sakes alone.

In other words there are things we enjoy which seem to have no survival value in the evolutionary struggle. We simply enjoy them. An artist produces a beautiful painting and I enjoy it 'for its own sake'. The painting brings me joy.

Roy Sambles, a physicist at the University of Exeter whose research team has pioneered studies of how light reflects from structured surfaces, has observed that although vivid blue Morpho butterflies from South America have an iridescent beauty which attracts old and young alike, we cannot eat them or use them for survival in any helpful manner. Why then do people perceive them as beautiful and wonder at their form? Even stranger, why do most of us see the barren frozen wasteland of the Antarctic as 'awesomely beautiful' as Simon Jenkins put it in an article published in *The Times* in January 2003? Surely such an inhospitable place which has little or no food for us, and in which we have virtually no chance of survival should be frightening, but our actual responses are quite the reverse. Beauty, awe and wonder do not sit happily with your view that evolution by natural selection explains our existence.

Here we speak of mysteries. Perhaps God's purposes in creating the world – let us forget the universe for a moment – included the coming into being of values among people in community. Genesis 2:18 has God saying, 'It is not good that the man should be alone; I will make him a helper as his partner.' This suggests God's purpose. We are most fulfilled when we know and love one another and love him. Relationships are good. Relationships reflect a 'personal' God (even though he certainly transcends what we understand by personal).

So, I should aim at goodness because that is the purpose of my existence. Leaving aside the question of whether I can achieve goodness without the grace of God, the point is that, for the Christian, purpose is real and rooted in the mind of the Creator of the universe. I should follow that purpose because I can see that it is a good purpose which can and will be realized, and also because in doing so I have a chance of enjoying one of the greatest human blessings – an obedient relationship of love with God.

The Apostle Paul reminded Christians in the church at Ephesus that, 'we are God's workmanship, created in Christ Jesus to do good works, which God prepared in advance for us to do' (Ephesians 2:10). Christians believe that the reasons why God created the universe include the admiration and appreciation of goodness, beauty and truth. We listen to an orchestra playing a magnificent piece of music. We glimpse these values now.

Scientific investigation itself can only proceed if the universe appears to make some sense to us. Religious believers may say to scientists, many of whom are believers, and to themselves, 'God has created us to understand and revere creation; therefore let's seek truth as vigorously as we can.' We live in a world where there are values. As we look at human life we see value, a sense of moral obligation, beauty and culture. The existence of God would explain this. Whereas natural selection, *on its own* – even at the genetic level at which biologists now understand it – leaves unexplained all the phenomena of consciousness, freedom and purpose that characterize human life.

Christians believe that all human beings have some sort of moral impulse, a reflection of the good God who created us. It is a point the force of which does not depend on an acceptance of the validity of the Bible. But it is a biblical argument, as when Paul spoke of non-Jews who 'do not possess the law' but 'do instinctively what the law requires'. They show that 'what the law requires is written on their hearts, to which their own conscience also bears witness'.

The Christian idea of God

Christian theology never portrays God as a created being. Christians believe that God is eternal. He has neither beginning nor end. Nothing could bring into being a reality who is necessarily what he is. He cannot help existing.

God is outside time in what theologians call his transcendence but he interacts with the universe in what theologians call his immanence. Modern physics has made this easier to understand when it tells us that we may consider time as a dimension with similar characteristics to space, both of which began at the big bang. So we may view God as existing outside our space–time dimension but simultaneously interacting with our world of space and time in his creative activity.

He is beyond speech and description, beyond being as we can understand it, without limit or boundary. He has brought order out of disorder, light from darkness. He is the God of the whole universe, whose knowledge and upholding of every elementary particle at every moment (from our space–time perspective) is complete and absolute.

And so the voice of God in creation gave rise to laws of nature. The intelligible order that we see around us depends on the word of God as its source and ground. He is responsible for the fundamental laws of the universe and set it on its course towards the creation of the galaxies and life itself. Yet he upholds every moment by his presence, and without him no time would exist. He is active in the world, providing for the needs of his creatures.

God created the universe for a purpose. He is worshipped as the supremely perfect being of whom everything else that is good is a reflection.

The Genesis account of creation

You dismiss the Genesis story as one of many creation myths. In my view, there is a majesty, beauty and a depth of insight in the opening chapters of Genesis which has stood the test of time. You like to paint a picture of many generations of Christians holding to a naively literal interpretation of the Bible until Darwin comes along with his theory of evolution. You then go on to suggest that, in the years following publication of *The Origin of Species*, liberal Christians and trendy bishops developed less fundamentalist ideas to accommodate evolution within their theology. This is a quite inaccurate version of what has happened.

Jewish and Christian scholars have from earliest centuries understood that the early chapters of Genesis contain figurative language that can only be understood in its original context. Way back in AD 231, Origen, the most important theologian and biblical scholar of the early Greek church, commenting on the first chapters of Genesis, wrote: 'I do not think anyone will doubt that these are figurative expressions which indicate mysteries through a semblance of history.'[143]

And towards the end of the fourth century, Augustine wrote, in his commentary on Genesis: 'In the case of a narrative of events, the question arises as to whether everything must be taken according to the figurative sense only, or whether it must be expounded and defended also as a faithful record of what happened. No Christian would dare to say that the narrative must not be taken in a figurative sense.'[144] He went on to suggest that the days of creation were not periods of time but rather categories that the author used in order to produce an understandable description of the work of creation.

The opening chapters of Genesis are certainly not a scientific treatise. They amount to a magnificent essay describing in a few strokes of the pen how God created the heavens and the earth and the Spirit of God hovered over the waters. It was a sovereign creation *ex nihilo* ('out of nothing'). There is no eternal matter or eternal evil spirit. The sun is a mere creature, not a god. God created the whole of reality including time.

When God said, 'Let there be,' his creative commands gave rise to orderly sequences and enduring structures in the world of time and space. According to Genesis 1, on the third day, at God's command, the land produces vegetation: 'seed-bearing plants' – in other words the plants possess within themselves the capacity, apparently on their own, to reproduce similar plants. Similarly he creates trees bearing fruit *with seed in it* (Genesis 1:11).

On the fifth day, again at God's command, the waters teem with living creatures and birds fly in the sky. God sees that it is all good. God blesses these sea creatures and birds and tells them to be fruitful and increase in number and fill the water in the sea and the sky above.

The sixth day is an especially busy day for God. The words of his commands are interesting: *Let the land produce* living creatures – livestock, creatures that move along the ground, and wild animals each according to their kind. But then the language changes: no longer are the words 'let the land produce' or 'let the waters teem'. Instead we read, 'And God said, "Let us make man in our image, in our likeness . . ."' (v. 26). The use of language here is well suited to the idea of evolution. All living creatures have an origin which is from one angle natural and from another supernatural; the natural process will appear to be self-perpetuating and autonomous, even though it will be

God's continuing work of creation. Fertility is a created capacity from the hand of the one God.

The man is set apart from the animals first by his office: 'let them rule . . .' (1:26) and in the second chapter when God brings the animals to Adam to be named (2:19). But man's crowning glory is his relation to God, who makes him 'in our image, in our likeness'. Even after the fall of man, he is still said to be in God's image (e.g. Genesis 9:6).

As long as we are human we are, according to Genesis, in the image of God. But the spiritual likeness – in a single word, love ('God is love') – can only be seen when God and man are in fellowship. The Fall damaged the image but our redemption recreates and perfects it.

The implications of the biblical idea that we are made in the image and likeness of God exclude the idea that our Creator is the 'wholly Other'; and requires us to take all human beings infinitely seriously.

A second and more detailed account of the creation of man in Genesis 2 tells us in verse 7 how 'the Lord God formed the man from the dust of the ground and breathed into his nostrils the breath of life, and the man became a living being'. This verse has a profound simplicity which matches the classic poetry of the first description in 1:27. The idea of God 'forming' the man from the dust of the ground does carry implications of skill and design (and see Psalm 94:9 'Does he who formed the eye not see?'). The biblical idea that we are 'designed' by the Creator also comes across in Psalm 139:14: 'I am fearfully and wonderfully made; your works are wonderful . . . My frame was not hidden from you when I was made in the secret place. When I was woven together in the depths of the earth, your eyes saw my unformed body.'

The idea of God *breathing* is warmly personal with all the face-to-face intimacy of a kiss. In the book of Job it is recorded that one of Job's friends, Elihu, reckoned that, 'it is the spirit in a man, the breath of the Almighty, that gives him understanding' (Job 32:8).

Other expressions of Genesis 2 place man in his earthly setting, since he is as truly natural as supernatural: a creation of common chemicals *from the ground* like the animals (2:19) and *a living being* as they are.

The man is placed in the garden of Eden. God shelters him but he does not smother him: on all sides discoveries and encounters await him to draw out his powers of discernment and choice. There are trees which are pleasing to the eye with fruit to eat to feed his *aesthetic* and *physical* appetite.

For his *spiritual* awakening, since he is made in God's image, he is given a divine word, double-edged, to live by. He is *free* to eat the fruit of any tree in the garden (v. 16) but he *must not* eat from the tree of the knowledge of good and evil (v. 17). He is given both freedom and responsibility. The animals have no such capacity and no such charge. The man is called to set a course and to hold to it.

He has work to do to take care of the garden. In modern terms, he is a steward of the environment around him, with a responsibility to look after it. This idea is taken up in Psalm 8 where David uses language of which you thoroughly disapprove in attempting to answer the question 'What is man?' In a prayerful song of praise, he tells the Lord 'You made [man] ruler over the works of your hands; you put everything under his feet: all flocks and herds, and the beasts of the field, the birds of the air, and the fish of the sea, all that swim the paths of the seas.'

The reference in Genesis 1:12 to gold, aromatic resin and onyx hints at the world's mineral resources. The man is going to have a big creative task on his hands, and this is seen in part as a blessing, although it will also be hard work.

And then there is the theme of human relationships. Companionship is presented in Eden as a primary human need: 'It is not good for the man to be alone' (2:18). God meets this need by creating not Adam's duplicate but his opposite and complement and by uniting the two, male and female, in harmony. The first signs of this harmony breaking down appear, not when Adam and Eve have an argument, but when they agree together against God. Without obedience to God, love is less than perfect. Genesis shows some happy relationships and some stormy ones, including violence and even murder.

The Christian idea of creation

You have managed to associate the prestige of the theory of evolution with your personal ideology that there is no God. The result is that in the media and in public perception the two ideas are frequently associated together. You also seem to want people to believe that if something can be explained in scientific terms then it can no longer be regarded as created by God. The converse of this view, which appears to be held by some Christians who may not be thinking clearly enough, is that if something cannot currently be explained and is rather mysterious, then this is the particular area of faith or religion.

Actually when the Bible writers speak of God's work in creation, they nearly always do so not by invoking the spooky and the mysterious, but by reminding their readers of God's creative actions in the mundane and ordinary events of everyday life: seed-time and harvest, stormy winds fulfilling God's command, the lion seeking its food from God, God making the grass grow for the cattle, and so on. In many passages in the book of Job, the Psalms and Isaiah the writers are not looking for God at the edges of the known world, least of all in their gaps in understanding, but pointing to his daily actions in familiar events.

The Creator has never stopped breathing life into the world and continues to sustain it moment by moment. You are familiar with Dr Arthur Peacocke, currently Warden Emeritus at the Society of Ordained Scientists and Honorary Chaplain and Canon at Christ Church Cathedral in Oxford. A biochemist, Peacocke believes that evolution can enhance our understanding of the Judeo-Christian God. He notes that evolution is compatible with the Christian idea of *creatio continua*, that God is continuously creating. Creation is not 'something that God did once in the past, and then walked off . . . It's something that's going on all the time.'[145]

We can think of creation as a seamless cloth of God's activity. An episode of *EastEnders* on the TV depends on the continual targeting of electrons onto the screen to generate the necessary images. If the flow of electrons ceased, there would be no drama. In the same way, there would be no scientists and nothing for scientists to describe if God, the author of the drama, ceased his ongoing creative and sustaining activity. The author of the drama allows the actors a certain amount of free will – which complicates the plot. And just to complete the analogy, if we were not living in an orderly universe, with known laws, the TV screen would look more like a snowstorm than *EastEnders*, just as it does when something has gone wrong with the signal.

What do we mean by 'nature'?

The biblical writers make no distinction between the 'natural' and the 'supernatural'; indeed the word 'supernatural' never occurs in the Bible.

Moreover, the Hebrew word *bārā*, which in English Bibles is translated 'create' in Genesis 1:1, 21 and 27 is also used, for example, in Psalm 104:24–30 and other places for a 'natural' process.

How many are your works, O Lord!
In wisdom you made them all;
the earth is full of your creatures.
There is the sea, vast and spacious,
teeming with creatures beyond number –
living things both large and small.
There the ships go to and fro,
and the leviathan, which you formed to frolic there.
These all look to you
to give them their food at the proper time.
When you give it to them,
they gather it up;
when you open your hand,
they are satisfied with good things.
When you hide your face,
they are terrified;
when you take away their breath,
they die and return to the dust.
When you send your Spirit,
they are created,
and you renew the face of the earth.

This illustrates how the Bible writers make no clear distinction between creation by a process and creation without process. Certainly they were convinced that at various times and places unusual events occurred, but they perceived all events without exception to be in God's hands.

Augustine said, 'Nature is what God does.' The earliest members of the Royal Society in the seventeenth century believed that nature represented God's creative activities. Nature is therefore intelligible and created both to be understood by humans and to serve their needs. Natural philosophy is an aspect of worship. And the human brains that can generate the language used in science and all branches of learning are also a part of God's created order.

Aubrey Moore (1843–90), theologian, Fellow of St John's College, Oxford, and curator of the Oxford Botanical Gardens, wrote: 'There are not, and cannot be, any Divine interpositions in nature, for God cannot interfere with Himself, His creative activity is present everywhere. There is no division of labour between God and nature, or God and law . . . For the Christian theologian the facts of nature are the acts of God.'[146] It was Moore who shrewdly pointed out that any 'creationist' doctrine that God occasionally intervenes in the ordinary processes of nature, for example, to create a new species, implies that God is ordinarily absent from nature and separate from it.[147]

What does 'automatic' mean?

You often talk about 'processes of automatic selection between rival molecules' when you describe how natural selection works. How may we understand this 'automatic' process?

When Jesus tells the parable of the growing seed, recorded in Mark 4, he describes a man who scatters seed on the ground. 'Night and day, whether he sleeps or gets up, the seed sprouts and grows, though he does not know how. *All by itself* the soil produces corn – first the stalk, then the ear, then the full grain in the ear' (Mark 4:28). The Greek word translated 'all by itself' is the word *automatos*. Jesus is recognizing that a process which he of all people would attribute to God's activity can take place, in one sense, *all by itself*. Triggered by light, heat and moisture, the seed contains within itself all that is needed to grow. But the process may still be sustained by God. Words like 'automatic' do not eliminate the idea of the hand of God.

Analogy

The biblical idea of gaining insight from the world of nature is intriguing. When Jesus used a parable or other analogy drawn from nature or humanity, it was not just an illustration, it was also a demonstration of something deeper. To be sure, these analogies help to make the truth intelligible or vivid, but their power is deeper in the sense that there is a harmony between the natural and spiritual worlds. When Paul wrote to the members of the church he had founded in Corinth he referred the miracle of sowing and reaping by which a small seed is transformed into a plant. 'Someone will ask,' Paul writes, 'how are the dead raised? With what kind of body do they come? Fool! What you sow does not come to life unless it dies. And as for what you sow, you do not sow the body that is to be, but a bare seed. But God gives it a body as he has chosen, and to each kind of seed its own body' (1 Corinthians 15:35–38).

For the New Testament writers, things on Earth seem to have been copies of things in Heaven. The decaying seed in the earth, rising up from death to become a graceful stalk, is a picture of the final resurrection. All the world with its rulers and subjects, its parents and children, its sun and moon, its sowing and harvest, its light and darkness, its sleeping and waking, its birth and death, is a powerful parable, a teaching of spiritual truth to help us in our journey into faith and understanding.

Revelation

In *The Blind Watchmaker*, you tell us why you reject the theory that life was created, or its evolution master-minded, by a conscious designer. 'Theory' is your word, but neither Christians, Jews nor Muslims think of their beliefs as a theory but as something which has been revealed in various ways by God himself.

You assert that Christians simply postulate the existence of a complex creator God without telling us who caused him in the first place. Now, no believer in God 'postulates' his existence. God is not a hypothesis. Christianity is not an explanation that is offered for debate as a rival to other theories which may have some bearing on our existence. You constantly assess religion on its merits as a rival to science as an explanation of the world around us.

According to both the Bible and history, God has satisfied humanity's quest for understanding by revealing his divine power and will to men and women so that we may come to know him. In any human relationship there is a certain amount we can learn from watching a person's behaviour and appearance, but this does not begin to compare with what we can know if a person is willing to open himself up to us and share his thoughts.

If we are to get to know God, it is necessary that he should reveal to us who he is rather than allowing us to remain in the dark. The revelation of God in Scripture is personal. He reveals his name. He enters into a covenant with us, and gives himself to be known by us.

God's word to his people through the prophet Jeremiah was: 'I will put my laws in their minds and write it on their hearts. I will be their God, and they will be my people. No longer will a man teach his neighbour, or a man his brother, saying, "Know the Lord," because they will all know me, from the least of them to the greatest,' (Jeremiah 31:33–34). He comes to us in categories of thought and action which make sense to us.

Psalm 19 has two types of revelation. On the one hand, 'the heavens are telling the glory of God' in such a way that it is impossible for anyone not to know it. On the other hand, there is a message for the people of Israel which conveys specific information about the gift and demands of God. God is the source of both types of revelation, 'general' and 'special', which work towards the same goal.

God gave his law through Moses, and speaks to us through Jesus Christ, along with apostles and prophets. God's acts are made more meaningful because they are accompanied by verbal commentary which give us insight into the character and purposes of the Creator.

God not only raises the crucified Christ from the dead, but he also explains to us the redemptive significance of the action. 'Christ died for our sins,' Paul writes, 'according to the Scriptures' (1 Corinthians 15:3). And so God has ensured that his revelation has been written down in words in the Bible. It would be surprising if this were not so, given the linguistic ability of humans.

Scripture is God's verbal revelation in writing. The Bible is a record of God revealing himself on the public stage of history in a series of events that are both predicted and explained. Many have already occurred, such as the birth, death and resurrection of Jesus and the outpouring of the Spirit at Pentecost. One of the facts of history that you have to account for is the birth and massive growth of the Christian church. The final climax of the story will be Christ's return for judgement and cosmic renewal which will end history as we know it.

Of course not everyone gets the message. 'I praise you, Father, Lord of heaven and earth,' Jesus prayed on one occasion, 'because you have hidden these things from the wise and learned, and revealed them to little children' (Matthew 11:25). However the Creator of light itself also illuminates individual hearts, as Paul reminded the members of the church in Corinth: 'For God, who said, "Let light shine out of the darkness," made his light shine in our hearts to give us the light of the knowledge of the glory of God in the face of Christ' (2 Corinthians 4:6). This same Paul, incidentally, was anxious to point out that the message he preached was neither made up nor received second hand: 'I received it by revelation from Jesus Christ' (Galatians 1:12); and told new Christians in Ephesus that he was praying that God 'will give you the Spirit of wisdom and revelation, so that you may know him better' (Ephesians 1:17).

Logos and creation

The Greek term '*Logos*', which is often translated in the Bible 'the word', speaks of both communication and reason. The idea of the *Logos* is an ancient concept in philosophy. It conveys the idea of a unifying, rational principle which holds together the world in a state of flux. The term often denotes the instrument by which the world was created; and it represents a bridge between God and the material world. The prophets speak of 'the word of the Lord' which they pass on to the people. In the New Testament, the writer to the Hebrews talks about God speaking through his Son by whom the world was created.

John, in his gospel, refers to Jesus as the Word, the agent of creation and the source of life and 'light that gives light to every man' (John 1:9). Jesus is the fullest way in which God has made himself known to men and women. His life, his teaching and his character portray God, for he was God living as a man. Jesus has intrigued people for two thousand years by what he said and did – every thoughtful person ought, I think, to reach a verdict on his unique claims.

The Apostle Paul told a noisy crowd in Derbe that God has 'not left himself without testimony' (Acts 14:17) and, in his letter to Christians in Rome, remarked that ever since the creation of the world, God's 'eternal power and divine nature' had been understood through the things he has made.

Evidence for the resurrection

In your interview with *Third Way* magazine, when Nick
Pollard suggested to you that there is solid evidence for
the resurrection of Jesus, you replied,

> I think you are on dangerous ground. There have been many
> people who allege that they see fairies. The fact is that we just
> don't believe them. We think they're hallucinating, or lying.
> Now, I don't know where the story of Jesus rising from the
> dead comes from. The actual documentary evidence is very
> bad as historical evidence goes, and so, given its enormous
> inherent implausibility, I'd be much more inclined to suspect
> it. You needn't go as far as to say 'hoax' – it's just that when
> very, very charismatic people die, legends grow up about
> them in a very mysterious way.

I cannot let you get away with your assertion that
documentary evidence for the resurrection is poor. The
facts are that about five thousand Greek manuscripts of
the New Testament exist in whole or in part. The most
important of these go back to somewhere around AD 350,
the two best being the Codex Vaticanus, the chief treasure
of the Vatican Library in Rome, and the Codex Sinaiticus,
which the British Government bought from the Soviet
Government in 1933 and which is now one of the most
prized exhibits in the British Museum. Other important
early manuscripts of the New Testament are held in the
British Museum and Cambridge University Library.

Now compare this happy situation with the textual
material we hold as evidence for other ancient historical
works. For Caesar's *Gallic War* (composed between 58 and
50 BC) there are several manuscripts, but only nine or ten
are good, and the oldest is some nine hundred years later
than Caesar's day. I could go on to make similar points
about the works of Livy, Tacitus, Thucydides and so on but

I expect I would try your patience (although you did tell one interviewer that you are interested in biblical studies and literature). The point is that the documentary evidence for the New Testament is very much more reliable than for other famous historical writings which no one ever questions.

In addition to the two excellent fourth-century manuscripts I have referred to, there are considerable fragments remaining of papyrus copies of books of the New Testament which are dated from one hundred to two hundred years earlier still. One very early fragment of a papyrus codex containing John 18:31–33, 37f., now in the John Rylands Library in Manchester, has been dated to around AD 130, showing that the Gospel of John was already circulating in Egypt about forty years after it was written.

Christians see the resurrection as both a miracle and a fact of history: if the event did not happen, certain recorded events are inexplicable. How do you account for the change in the disciples from fear to courageous joy unless the one whom they knew had been crucified rose from the dead? If he did not rise, why did the religious or civil authorities in Jerusalem not produce and parade the dead body to put a stop to the rapid growth of the early church as the disciples preached Jesus and the resurrection?

Paley and the role of natural theology

From Thomas Aquinas to William Paley, many theologians and Christian writers tried to show that certain features of the world indicated that belief in God was rational, indeed the only belief which can make sense of things. They were not attempting to produce 'knockdown' arguments for God any more than I am. However, it seems reasonable for Christians to assume that if God is the Creator the world will reveal its maker.

In 1986, you chose the title of your book *The Blind Watchmaker* because of the famous illustration used by William Paley in his book *Natural Theology, or Evidences of the Existence and Attributes of the Deity* (1802).

Paley believed that human beings are so remarkable that they must have a maker and sustainer. To convey this idea he used the analogy of the watch, which has proved popular even if it has not always been fashionable to agree with it.

Suppose I am crossing a heath, Paley suggested, and I kick my foot against a stone. Someone might ask me how the stone came to be there and I might answer that, as far as I know, it has been there forever. But suppose I find a watch on the ground. If someone asks me how the watch happens to be there, I shall hardly repeat the same answer. Yet why, asks Paley, should this answer not suffice for the watch as well as for the stone? For this reason: that when we come to inspect the watch, we see that its various parts are made and put together for a purpose. That is, they are designed to produce motion, and that motion is so regulated that it indicates the time of day.

When we examine the mechanism of the watch we decide that it must have had a maker who understood its construction and designed its use. If we subsequently discovered that the watch sometimes went wrong or that it seldom went exactly right, our initial conclusion would remain unchallenged.

It would not be sufficient explanation, says Paley, to be told that there exists in the universe a 'principle of order' that had placed the parts of the watch in their present shape and position. 'I never knew a watch made by the principle of order,' Paley noted wryly. Nor, he said, could he distinguish in his mind between what is meant by a principle of order and the intelligence of the watchmaker.

Paley also wrote that he would be surprised to be told that the watch in his hand was no more than the result of the laws of *metallic* nature. 'It is a perversion of language to assign any law, as the efficient, operative cause of anything. A law presupposes an agent; for it is only the mode, according to which an agent proceeds: it implies a power; for it is the order, according to which that power acts.'[148]

You are happy to admit that you admire the archdeacon of Carlisle. 'Paley had a point to make,' you wrote in *The Blind Watchmaker*, 'he passionately believed in it and spared no effort to ram it home clearly. He had a proper reverence for the complexity of the living world and realised that it demands a very special kind of explanation. His descriptions of that complexity were good, especially in the light of the scientific knowledge of his day. However his explanation of the complexity and of the indications of design in the world were wrong – gloriously and utterly wrong!'[149]

You insist that the analogy Paley drew between watch and living organism is false: 'All appearances to the contrary, the only watchmaker in nature is the blind forces of physics, albeit deployed in a very special way.'[150]

I think that in assessing Paley it is easy to forget that, although he is often dismissed as 'an eighteenth-century clergyman' (or words to that effect), his contemporaries regarded him as the cleverest man of his generation, who won the coveted senior wranglership at Cambridge and other prizes. When I read his books I am impressed by the urbanity of his style and the nuanced sophistication of his reasoning. Orthodox Christians may be grateful that he did an important job in opposing the deists who denied God's continuing providential action. The real truth, he believed, was that the universe worked by the continuing power of God. Even an occasional intervention was a poor substitute for a continuously active Creator. He was not content with a God who stood offstage.

In addition to his religious interests, Paley was a keen and careful naturalist, and his books contain many fine descriptions of organic structures and their adaptation to the environment (you have paid tribute to this). He was well aware of evolutionary ideas (though of course lived too early to come to terms with natural selection as the mechanism). His analogy of the watch does not actually rule out some sort of evolutionary development because his watch was itself the result of a process. It could not have arrived fully formed into the world just like that: it had a traceable history. Generations of watchmakers selected those basic principles which would create a device to tell the time. They tried and discarded lots of versions of timepieces until they finally refined the mechanisms of the watch that Paley described. Less efficient versions – water clocks, pendulums, marked candles – were confined to museums.

When he set out his analogy of the watch he carefully anticipated a whole series of possible objections to it including the scenario that on examining the watch it 'is found, in the course of its movement, to produce another watch, similar to itself; and not only so, but we perceive in it a system of organisation, separately calculated for that purpose. What effect would this discovery have, or ought it to have, upon our former inference? What, as has been already said, but to increase beyond measure, our admiration of the skill which had been employed in the formation of such a machine?'[151] My hunch is that Paley would have readily embraced natural selection within his Christian understanding.

God speaks today

God continues to speak today. Christians say that you can hear his voice through human friendship, through music and the arts and through our appreciation and love of all that is beautiful, good and true. Christ's followers are given the Holy Spirit who speaks to individuals and churches and transforms those who listen to him.

Believers try to know, love and trust him and have learnt to do so in communities founded by monks, missionaries and mystics who have claimed to experience something of the reality of God. He may be encountered in fellowships of Christians meeting in lofty churches or suburban houses. Believers may be encouraged by glimpses of eternity in their own lives. They often try to pass on the good news to others, even if anxiously and falteringly. A sense of the reality of God may lead to the birth of religious faith in an unbeliever.

All over the world, believers are convinced they experience answers to prayer. They have to work at it. Often they find prayer a perplexing mystery. But still they are inclined to say with another Wallace – John not Alfred – the Scottish hymn writer, 'Prayer moves the hand that moves the world.'

The nature of truth

Jesus taught once in the Jerusalem temple in the middle of the Feast of Tabernacles. Astonished at the nature and content of his teaching, his audience asked where Jesus had acquired his wisdom when he had never been taught. The Lord replied that his teaching came from God and that anyone who resolved to be obedient to God would know whether his teaching was genuine (John 7:17).

Here understanding is a consequence of obedience. Some truths can only be understood and appreciated by personal commitment. Knowledge of such truths transforms the knower. Spiritual truth is of that kind.

Scientists should be more open to truth than those who are not so aware of the awe-inspiring structure of the universe. Often they have been. Great scientists like

Newton, Faraday, Maxwell and Einstein may not always have been orthodox believers, but they often showed an awareness – and sometimes a strong conviction – of a vast intelligence underlying the universe, and a reverence before the mystery of our existence. The best science has its own form of contemplation, an awesome delight at the beauty and complexity of the world.

10

The Mystery of Suffering

In your view there is no overriding purpose for good underlying the universe. There is just nature and DNA. And nature is not cruel, just indifferent. You think we find it hard to accept this. We cannot bring ourselves to admit that things might be neither good nor evil, neither cruel nor kind, but simply indifferent to all suffering, lacking any purpose. You say that DNA survival is not about happiness. In the process of evolution, so long as DNA is passed on, it does not matter who or what gets hurt in the process.

Darwin could not fathom why a loving God should create a type of wasp who loved to eat a caterpillar alive. You say it is better for the genes of the wasp that the caterpillar should be alive, and therefore fresh, when it is eaten, no matter what the cost in suffering. Genes do not care about suffering, because they do not care about anything. If nature were kind, she would make sure that caterpillars were anaesthetized before they were eaten. But for you, nature is neither kind nor unkind. She is neither against suffering nor for it. Her business is simply the survival of DNA. And DNA just is. So you are not surprised that we experience suffering.

Hundreds of books have been written on the problem of suffering (for it does perplex believers in a loving God) but we still get toothache – or much worse. In the Christian tradition scholars try to tackle the question of 'theodicy': *Si*

Deus justis – unde malum? (If God is righteous, why evil?).
No sensible Christian begins to think he knows the
answers but some helpful things have been said.

First, pain, though it hurts, is often not wholly evil. The
stab of pain acts as an alarm. All biological organisms have
complex warning signals that communicate both external
and internal dangers. Our survival depends on our
possession of pain receptors – otherwise we would not be
here. Without pain receptors we would be eating with
decayed teeth, walking on broken ankles, getting
extremely sunburnt and ignoring heart attacks. Perhaps
we can go on to say that living with pain can purge, refine
even ennoble character. In this sense pain may be a gift and
a mercy.

Second, from a Christian perspective, virtue (choosing
good) is only possible where vice (choosing evil) is also
possible. I speak of mysteries way beyond me here and I
put the point crudely: but what were God's options when
he created men and women? I suppose he could have
created a world of robots – but a robot's programmed
performance cannot be virtuous in this sense and lacks the
value of virtue. In making men and women capable of
choosing the path of grateful obedience to him, he made
them capable of not doing so. Though not sin's author,
God created a possibility of sin by creating the possibility
of righteousness.

Somehow the freedom God gives us seems to give rise
to the possibility of suffering. Using their freedom, and the
sophisticated form of consciousness which is uniquely
theirs, humans choose to pursue sexual pleasure, thrills
and competitive activities. They prefer to do their own
thing, be courageously adventurous and take risks. These
activities involve the risk of suffering. This is not to
suggest that God punishes us for behaving like this; it is
simply to observe some sort of link between freedom, self-
awareness, selfishness and suffering.

There seems to be a link between self-indulgence and suffering – although I would not put this forward as an answer to the problem of pain. To give two obvious examples: if one evening I enjoy the most marvellous seven-course meal accompanied by an unlimited supply of the best wines, I wake up the next morning with acute stomach-ache and a blinding headache. My suffering is the result of my self-indulgent pursuit of happiness the previous evening. More seriously, if a man leaves his wife of thirty years to enjoy a passionate relationship with a beautiful twenty-year-old woman, his wife and children are likely to experience intense unhappiness – or, to put it another way, innocent suffering.

Third, moral growth and maturity are only possible when the consequences of our actions are calculable. If God means this world to be a school for moral growth he gives it physical regularity so that consequences may be foreseen. Frustrations through miscalculation, and natural events called disasters because they damage humans, are therefore inevitable. Sometimes we mature morally through coping with them.

In her book *The Experience of Childbirth*, Sheila Kitzinger has described a link between creativity and pain. She speaks of the pain of childbirth as a side-effect of the creative process, of muscles tightening and stretching as the baby's head presses down to be born – positive pain, pain with a purpose.

The Bible itself attempts to tackle the problem of suffering in the ancient book of Job. When the Lord eventually speaks to Job 'through the storm' he gives him no explanation of his suffering. Instead he gives him a glimpse of his greatness and infinite wisdom especially as seen in creation. Although we may sometimes think we understand a little of a purpose in suffering, God's ways are so much higher than ours that his full purposes are always beyond us. Many of our explanations are just words. It would be better if we kept silent. I do not have you in mind when I write this, since you do not attempt to explain suffering. You think it just is and you are not surprised.

To those who blame God for suffering, we can say, 'Look at the cross, the heart of the Christian faith.' The creator is also a God who suffers in Christ his Son. Old Testament prophets looked forward to Christ as the 'suffering servant'.

The theological idea of the 'self-emptying of God' – *kenosis* – based on the Greek of Philippians 2:7 (*kenoō* God emptying himself, making himself nothing) is that of a God who gives himself to overcome evil and create salvation through death and resurrection. As part of the mystery of God, the Creator of time accepts the experience of our temporal existence, and makes himself vulnerable. The suffering Christian may be sustained by the thought that Christ not only suffered for his people but also suffered with them.

On the one hand, it obviously is not the Creator's purpose to prevent all suffering or preserve us from every type of harm. On the other hand, we see evidence of purpose almost everywhere in the universe. And we are not indifferent either to suffering or to goodness in the world. You have spoken of being close to tears when delivering a eulogy in memory of a deceased colleague. Listen to the callers to any radio phone-in programme: they are often desperately concerned to speak about what is right, what is wrong and how evil may be averted. But goals of value – like truth, beauty and goodness – often seem to be achieved in painful ways.

In heaven, earth's evils will in retrospect seem trivial. 'I consider,' observed the Apostle Paul, 'that our present sufferings are not worth comparing with the glory that will be revealed in us' (Romans 8:18).

The author of the book of Revelation describes a remarkable vision. He sees a great crowd of people 'from every nation, tribe, people and language' standing before the throne and of God. They are singing a song about salvation. There are lots of angels and living creatures worshipping God. In his vision, John is fortunate to have a friendly elder who is his guide and interpreter.

'These in white robes,' the elder asks John, 'who are they, and where did they come from?'

'Sir, you know,' John answers.

'They are they who have come out of the great tribulation,' the elder explains. 'They have washed their robes and made them white in the blood of the Lamb. Therefore, they are before the throne of God and serve him day and night in his temple; and he who sits on the throne will spread his tent over them. Never again will they hunger; never again will they thirst. The sun will not beat upon them, nor any scorching heat. For the Lamb at the centre of the throne will be their shepherd; he will lead them to springs of living water. And God will wipe away every tear from their eyes' (Revelation 7: 9, 13–17).

Christians believe that this is a universe in which the purposes of God are destined to be realized, so that – in some way that I cannot at the moment understand or appreciate – suffering creatures can be brought to experience the love and goodness which God wants to establish in his universe.

The nature of faith

You are scathing about religious faith. You argue that it is 'the great cop-out . . . blind trust, in the absence of evidence, even in the teeth of evidence'.[152] You have said that you think faith is a sort of mental illness causing people to do all sorts of foolish things and should therefore be avoided.

I think you either misunderstand or deliberately misrepresent the nature of Christian faith. Faith is not credulity. If I am credulous, I am gullible, uncritical, undiscerning and unreasonable in my beliefs. You are suggesting that faith and reason are incompatible. In the Bible faith and sight are set in opposition to each other, but not faith and reason. Faith is not a blind leap in the dark, but personal trust based on rational argument and the weighing of evidence.

Take the story of what happened on the evening of the Sunday on which Jesus rose from the dead. He appeared to ten disciples in the room of a house in Jerusalem. Thomas was not with them at the time and later the disciples told him 'We have seen the Lord.'

Thomas replied sceptically, insisting on evidence that the man they had grown to love, and had been crucified, was now alive again.

'Unless I see the mark of the nails in his hands,' Thomas told the other disciples, 'and put my finger in the mark of the nails and my hand in his side, I will not believe.'

A week later the disciples were again in the same house and this time Thomas was with them. Jesus joined them and, turning to Thomas, said: 'Put your finger here and see my hands. Reach out your hand and put it in my side. Do not doubt but believe.'

Jesus had respect for Thomas' demand for evidence. There was no expectation that the sceptical disciple should exercise blind trust in the absence of evidence. Thomas quickly responded with the words 'My Lord and my God!' (John 20:19–28).

Of course, generations of people since then have been invited to exercise faith without the privilege of sight granted to Thomas, but the point is that through the centuries followers of Christ have never been required to take a step – or make a leap – which is blind or irrational. Even in the Old Testament, when he tried to persuade the people to change their behaviour, the prophet Isaiah pleaded with them to reason with him. What I am saying makes sense, he implied: think about it. In the book of the Acts we read how the apostle Paul spent hours in the synagogues and public places arguing a rational case for the new religion of Christianity.

In the Sermon on the Mount, Jesus says: 'But if God so clothes the grass of the field, which is alive today and tomorrow is thrown into the oven, will he not much more clothe you – you of little faith?' (Matthew 6:30). Often the trouble with the person of little faith is that he does not think. Christian faith involves thought. Look at the birds, think about them and draw your conclusions. Look at the grass, look at the lilies of the field and consider them.

Thoughtful reflection on evidence has persuaded many initially hesitant people to commit themselves to the Christian faith: the evidence of beauty, harmony and design in the world about them; a conviction that the curious and sometimes unwelcome nagging of conscience within can be none other than the voice of God; a consideration of the life, character, words, impact, death and resurrection of Jesus; and reflection on the birth, growth and survival of the Christian church. Only reason and faith together can bring people to maturity.

A warning

A few days ago I was talking to a friend about this letter. He holds a chair in physics in a British university and believes that what we call the 'laws of nature' are upheld by the Creator who is described in Scripture and encountered in the lives of contemporary believers. He told me that he has a hunch; he put it no higher than that. He refused to describe it as a scientific hypothesis, even a working one. But his hunch is that one day you will become a Christian. It will mean the eclipse of the Damascus Road, but my friend and I both believe in miracles. You have been warned.

Yours sincerely

Roger Steer

P.S. You, or any other reader, can contact me via my website, www.rogersteer.com and I will be pleased to publish there all significant responses to the points I have made whether supportive or critical. I have placed at this site more details of some issues touched on above, including the anthropic principle, the 'just so universe', Monod's ideas about chance and necessity and 'intelligent design'.

P.P.S. I am grateful to the following people who helped and encouraged me in writing this letter: Denis Alexander, Sara Harnett, Roy Sambles, Hannah, Sheila and Tim Steer, and the team at Paternoster Publishing.

P.P.P.S. Best wishes to Juliet. I would love to know what she thinks today about those flowers.

Notes

1 Dear Professor Dawkins

1. Richard Dawkins, *Climbing Mount Improbable* (London: Penguin Books, 1977), p. 236.
2. Alfred R. Wallace, *The World of Life: A Manifestation of Creative Power, Directional Mind and Ultimate Purpose* (Chapman & Hall, 1910), p. 324.
3. Quoted by Denis Alexander in *Rebuilding the Matrix: Science and Faith in the 21st Century* (Oxford: Lion, 2001), p. 83.
4. Richard Dawkins, *The Blind Watchmaker* (London: Penguin, 1991), p. xiii.
5. This remark appeared on the dust cover of *The Blind Watchmaker*.
6. A.N. Wilson, *God's Funeral* (London: John Murray, 1999), p. 177.
7. Quoted in Alexander, *Rebuilding*, p. 85.
8. 'Science, delusion and the appetite for wonder', Richard Dimbleby Lecture given for BBC1 on 12 November 1996.

2 The mystery Darwin and Wallace set out to solve

9. Quoted by Michael Shermer, *The Life and Science of Alfred Russel Wallace: A Biographical Study on the Psychology of History* (Oxford: OUP, 2002), p. 57.
10. ibid., p. 82.
11. Quoted in Shermer, *Life and Science*, p. 102.
12. ibid., p. 105.

[13] Quoted in Peter Raby, *Alfred Russel Wallace: A Life* (London: Pimlico, 2002), p. 167.

[14] Charles Darwin, *The Origin of Species* (London: Everyman, 1928), p. 455.

[15] ibid.

[16] Edna Healey, *Emma Darwin* (London: Review, 2002), p. 279.

[17] ibid., p. 258.

[18] Charles Darwin, *The Descent of Man and Selection in Relation to Sex* (London: John Murray, 1899), p. 613.

[19] Adrian Desmond and James Moore, *Darwin* (London: Penguin, 1992), p. 636.

[20] ibid.

[21] ibid.

[22] Richard Dawkins, 'When religion steps on science's turf', Council for Secular Humanism, *Free Inquiry* 18:2 and at http://secularhumanism.org/library/fi/dawkins_18_2.html.

[23] Darwin, *Descent*, p. 613.

[24] ibid.

[25] Richard Dawkins, *River out of Eden* (London: Phoenix Books, 1995), p. 111.

[26] Vernon Blackmore and Andrew Page, *Evolution: The Great Debate* (Oxford: Lion, 1989), p. 118.

[27] Quoted in Alexander, *Rebuilding*, p. 332.

[28] ibid.

[29] Desmond and Moore, *Darwin*, p. 675.

[30] Victor Pearce, *Evidence for Truth: Science* (London: Eagle 1998), p. 163.

[31] Alexander, *Rebuilding*, p. 203.

3 Alfred Russel Wallace

[32] Shermer, *Life and Science*, p. 21.

[33] ibid., p. 53.

[34] ibid.

[35] ibid., p. 113.

[36] ibid., p. 118.

[37] ibid., p. 148.

[38] ibid., p. 13.

[39] ibid.

[40] ibid.

[41] ibid.

[42] Wallace, *The World of Life*, Preface.

[43] Shermer, *Life and Science*, p. 167.

[44] ibid., p. 169.

[45] Wallace, *The World of Life*, pp. 284–285.

[46] Shermer, *Life and Science*, p. 170.

[47] ibid.

[48] ibid.

[49] ibid.

[50] ibid.

[51] ibid., p. 171.

[52] ibid.

[53] ibid.

[54] ibid., p. 173.

[55] ibid., p. 173–174.

[56] Wallace, *The World of Life*, p. 337.

[57] ibid.

[58] ibid.

[59] Paul Davies, *The Fifth Miracle: The Search for the Origin of Life* (London: Penguin, 1997), p. 77.

[60] Alfred R. Wallace, *Darwinism: An Exposition of the Theory of Natural Selection with Some of its Applications* (London and New York: Macmillan, 1891), p. 447.

[61] Wallace, *The World of Life*, p. 188.

[62] ibid., p. 186.

[63] ibid., p. 325.

[64] ibid.

[65] ibid., p. 359.

[66] ibid., p. 365.

[67] ibid., p. 368.

[68] Quoted in Howard J. Van Till, 'Basil, Augustine, and the doctrine of creation's functional integrity', *Science and Christian Belief* (April 1996), p. 29.

[69] ibid., p. 333.

[70] ibid., pp. 186–187.

[71] Alfred R. Wallace, *Man's Place in the Universe* (London: Chapman & Hall, 1908), p. 310f.

[72] Shermer, *Life and Science*, p. 161.

[73] ibid.

[74] ibid.

[75] ibid.

[76] ibid.

[77] ibid., p. 160.

[78] Healey, *Emma Darwin*, p. 291.

[79] ibid., p. 292.

[80] Shermer, *Life and Science*, p. 185.

[81] ibid., p. 48.

[82] Raby, *Alfred Russel Wallace*, p. 136.

[83] ibid., p. 172.

[84] Wallace, *The World of Life*, p. 8.

[85] Wilfred Ward, 'Tennyson: A Reminiscence' in *Problems and Persons* (London: Longman Green, 1903), pp. 196–217.

[86] Raby, *Alfred Russel Wallace*, p. 233.

[87] ibid., p. 282.

[88] Dawkins, 'When religion steps on science's turf'.

[89] Darwin, *Descent*, pp.125–126.

[90] ibid.

[91] Susan Greenfield, *The Private Life of the Brain* (London: Penguin, 2000), p. 45.

4 Evolution today

[92] Neil Broom, *How Blind is the Watchmaker?* (Leicester: IVP, 2001), p. 151.

[93] Dawkins, *River*, p. 20.

[94] ibid., p. 22.

[95] Steven Rose, *Lifelines Biology, Freedom and Determinism* (London: Penguin, 1998), p. 140.

[96] Interview conducted by the organization Counterbalance, text at http://www.meta-library.net/transcript/dawk-frame.html.

[97] Dawkins, *The Blind Watchmaker*, p. 141.

[98] Richard Dawkins, *The Selfish Gene* (Oxford: OUP, 1976), p. 19.

[99] Rose, *Lifelines*, p. 5f.

[100] Quoted in Broom, *How Blind?*, p. 67.

[101] Richard Dawkins and Steven Pinker, 'Is science killing the soul?', *Guardian*/Dillons debate, 10 February 1999, *Edge* 53 (8 April 1999), and at http://www.edge.org/documents/archive/edge53.html.

5 What evolution explains

[102] 'At home with Richard Dawkins', Interview with Madeleine Pym, *Humanist News* (Sept. 2002).

[103] Jacques Monod, *Chance and Necessity* (London: Fontana, 1974), p. 96.

[104] Alexander, *Rebuilding*, p. 352.

[105] Howard Van Till, Basil, 'Augustine, and the doctrine of creation's functional integrity', *Science and Christian Belief* (April 1996).

[106] Dawkins, *River*, p. 155.

[107] Dawkins, *The Selfish Gene*, p. 24.

[108] Richard Dawkins interview with Ben Wattenberg for *Think Tank* series on PBS. Full transcript at http://www.pbs.org/thinktank/transcript410.html.

[109] Roger Penrose, *The Emperor's New Mind: Concerning Computers, Minds, and the Laws of Physics* (London: Vintage, 1990), pp. 537–538.

[110] 'Darwin's dangerous disciple', interview with Frank Miele, *Skeptic* 3:4 (1995), pp. 80–85.

[111] Quoted in Alexander, *Rebuilding*, p. 83.

[112] Dawkins, *The Selfish Gene*, p. 43.

6 The Mind's Complexity

[113] Quoted in Alexander, *Rebuilding*, p. 84.

[114] Quoted in Roger Steer, *Dream of Reality* (London: Hodder & Stoughton, 1993), p. 3.

[115] John Henry Newman, *The Idea of a University, edited with introduction and notes by I.T. Kerr* (Oxford: OUP, 1976), pp. 74–75.

[116] *The Times*, 11 December 2002.

7 Consciousness

[117] Dawkins, *The Selfish Gene*, p. 50.

[118] ibid., p. 59.

[119] Rose, *Lifelines*, p. 214.

[120] Penrose, *The Emperor's New Mind*, p. 532.

[121] Greenfield, *Private Life*, p. 47.

[122] ibid., p. 50.

[123] ibid., p. 185.

[124] Dietrich Bonhoeffer, *The Cost of Discipleship* (London: SCM, 1959), p. 79.

8 God and the universe

[125] Stephen Hawking,'Letter to the Editor: Time and the Universe', *American Scientist* 73 (1985), p. 12.

[126] Stephen Hawking, *The Universe in a Nutshell* (London: Bantam, 2001), p. 86.

[127] John D. Barrow and Frank J. Tipler, *The Anthropic Cosmological Principle* (Oxford: Oxford University Press, 1986).

[128] Alexander, *Rebuilding*, pp. 422–425.

[129] Penrose, *The Emperor's New Mind*, pp. 445–446.

[130] Quoted in Walter Bradley, 'The 'Just So' Universe', *Touchstone* (July/August 1999), p. 72.

[131] ibid.

[132] ibid.

[133] ibid.

[134] ibid.

[135] ibid.

9 God and baseball hats

[136] Dawkins, *The Selfish Gene*, p. 193.

[137] Alexander, *Rebuilding*, p. 253.

[138] 'Christianity: Church and education', *Encyclopaedia Britannica* (2001).

[139] E.J. Larson and L.W. Witham, 'Scientists are still keeping the faith', *Nature* 386 (1997), pp. 435–436.

[140] Interview for Channel 4, 15 August 1994.

[141] Interview with Nick Pollard conducted on 28 February 1995 and published in *Third Way* 18:3 (April 1995) and at http://www.damaris.org/olr/features/1999/dawkinsinterview.htm.

[142] Darwin, *Descent*, p. 612.

[143] Quoted in Alexander, *Rebuilding*, p. 320.

[144] ibid.

[145] Interview with Counterbalance, text at http://www.meta-library.net/transcript/dawk-frame.html.

[146] Quoted in Alexander, *Rebuilding*, p. 199.

[147] ibid. p. 177.

[148] William Paley, *Paley's Works: Consisting of Evidences of Christianity, Moral and Political Philosophy, Natural Theology and Horae Paulinae* (London: Thomas Tegg & Son, 1835), p. 2.

[149] ibid., p. 5

[150] ibid.

[151] ibid., p. 2.

10 The mystery of suffering

[152] From a lecture by Richard Dawkins extracted from *The Nullifidian* (Dec. 94), text at http://www.world-of dawkins.com/Dawkins/Work/Articles/1994 12religion.htm.

Bibliography

Alexander, Denis, *Rebuilding the Matrix: Science and Faith in the 21st Century* (Oxford: Lion, 2001)

—, *Does Evolution Have Any Religious Significance?*, Christians in Science booklet (Pitlochry: 1998)

Barrow, John D. and Frank J. Tipler, *The Anthropic Cosmological Principle* (Oxford: Oxford University Press, 1986)

Berry, Wendell, *Life is a Miracle: An Essay against Modern Superstition* (Washington: Counterpoint, 2000)

Blackmore, Vernon and Andrew Page, *Evolution: The Great Debate* (Oxford: Lion, 1989)

Bonhoeffer, Dietrich, *The Cost of Discipleship* (London: SCM, 1959)

Bradley, Walter L., 'The "Just So" Universe', *Touchstone* (July/August 1999), 70–75

Broom, Neil, *How Blind Is the Watchmaker?* (Leicester: InterVarsity, 2001)

Brown, Colin, *Philosophy and the Christian Faith* (Leicester: Tyndale, 1969)

Darwin, Charles, *The Descent of Man and Selection in Relation to Sex* (London: John Murray, 1899)

—, *The Origin of Species*, Everyman edn (London: J.M. Dent, 1928)

Davies, Paul, *The Fifth Miracle: The Search for the Origin of Life* (London: Penguin, 1999)

Dawkins, Richard, *The Selfish Gene* (Oxford: Oxford University Press, 1976)

—, *The Blind Watchmaker* (London: Penguin, 1988)

—, Interview with Sheena McDonald, broadcast on Channel 4, 15 August 1994

—, lecture extracted from *The Nullifidian* (Dec. 94), text at http://www.world-of-dawkins.com/Dawkins/Work/Articles/1994-12religion.htm.

—, *River out of Eden* (London: Phoenix, 1995)

—, Interview with Nick Pollard conducted on 28 February 1995 and published in *Third Way* 18:3 (April 1995) and at http://www.damaris.org/olr/features/1999/dawkinsinterview.htm

—, Interview with Frank Miele, *Skeptic* 3:4 (1995), 80–85

—, 'Science, delusion and the appetite for wonder', Richard Dimbleby Lecture given for BBC1 on 12 November 1996

—, *Climbing Mount Improbable* (London: Penguin, 1997)

—, Interview with Ben Wattenberg for *Think Tank* series on PBS (2002). Full transcript at http://www.pbs.org/thinktank/transcript410.html

—, 'At home with Richard Dawkins', Interview with Madeleine Pym, *Humanist News* (Sept. 2002)

—, Interview with Counterbalance, text at http://www.meta-library.net/transcript/dawk-frame.html

—, 'The improbability of God', Council for Secular Humanism, *Free Inquiry* 18:3 and at http://www.secularhumanism.org/library/fi/dawkins_18_3.html

—, 'When religion steps on science's turf', Council for Secular Humanism, *Free Inquiry* 18:2 and at http://www.secularhumanism.org/library/fi/dawkins_18_2.html

Dawkins, Richard and Steven Pinker, 'Is science killing the soul?', Guardian/Dillons debate, 10 February 1999, *Edge* 53 (8 April 1999) and at http://www.edge.org/documents/archive/edge53.html

Dembski, William A., *The Design Inference: Eliminating Chance Through Small Probabilities* (Cambridge: Cambridge University Press, 1998)

Desmond, Adrian and James Moore, *Darwin* (London: Penguin, 1992)

Dyson, Freeman, *Origins of Life* (Cambridge: Cambridge University Press, 1985)

Eigen, Manfred, *Steps towards Life: A Perspective on Evolution* (Oxford: Oxford University Press, 1992)

Encyclopaedia Britannica (2001), entry: 'Christianity: Church and education'

Ferguson, Sinclair B. and David F. Wright (eds), *New Dictionary of Theology* (Leicester: InterVarsity, 1988)

Greene, Brian, *The Elegant Universe* (London: Vintage, 2000)

Greenfield, Susan, *The Private Life of the Brain* (London: Penguin, 2000)

Gribbin, John, *Almost Everyone's Guide to Science* (London: Phoenix, 1999)

—, *The Little Book of Science* (London: Penguin, 1999)

Hawking, Stephen, 'Letter to the Editor: Time and the Universe', *American Scientist* 73 (1985)

—, *The Universe in a Nutshell* (London: Bantam, 2001)

Healey, Edna, *Emma Darwin: The Inspirational Wife of a Genius* (London: Review, 2002)

Johnson, Phillip E., and Denis O. Lamoureux, *Darwinism Defeated? The Johnson–Lamoureux Debate on Biological Origins* (Vancouver: Regent College Publishing, 1999)

Jones, Steve, *Almost Like a Whale: The Origin of Species Updated* (London: Black Swan, 1999)

Kidner, Derek, *Genesis: An Introduction and Commentary* (Leicester: Tyndale, 1967)

Kitzinger, Sheila, *The Experience of Childbirth* (London: Gollancz, 1962)

Larson, E.J. and L.W. Witham, 'Scientists are still keeping the faith', *Nature* 386 (1997), 435–436

Lewis, John (ed.), *Beyond Chance and Necessity: A Critical Inquiry into Professor Jacques Monod's Chance and Necessity* (London: The Teilhard Centre for the Future of Man, 1974)

Lewontin, Richard C., *Biology as Ideology: The Doctrine of DNA* (London: HarperCollins, 1992)

Magnusson, Magnus (ed.), *Chambers Biographical Dictionary* (London: Chambers, 1990)

Meyer, Stephen C., 'Word games: DNA, design and intelligence', *Touchstone* (July/August 1999), 44–50

Monod, Jacques, *Chance and Necessity* (London: Fontana, 1974)

Newman, John Henry, *The Idea of a University, edited with introduction and notes by I.T. Kerr* (Oxford: Oxford University Press, 1976)

Paley, William, *Paley's Works: Consisting of Evidences of Christianity, Moral and Political Philosophy, Natural Theology and Horae Paulinae* (London: Thomas Tegg & Son, 1835)

Pearce, Victor, *Evidence for Truth: Science* (London: Eagle, 1998)

Pearcey, Nancy, 'Design and the discriminating public', *Touchstone* (July/August 1999), 25–28

Penrose, Roger, *The Emperor's New Mind: Concerning Computers, Minds, and the Laws of Physics* (London: Vintage, 1990)

Polkinghorne, John, *One World: The Interaction of Science and Theology* (London: SPCK, 1986)

Poole, Michael and Richard Dawkins, 'The Poole-Dawkins debate', *Science and Christian Belief* (April 1994)

Raby, Peter, *Alfred Russel Wallace: A Life* (London: Pimlico, 2002)

Raven, C.E., *Organic Design: A Study of Scientific Thought from Ray to Paley* (Oxford: Oxford University Press, 1954)

Rose, Steven, *Lifelines Biology, Freedom and Determinism* (London: Penguin, 1998)

Shaw, Bernard, *Back to Methuselah*, The Works of Bernard Shaw, vol. 16 (London: Constable & Co Ltd, 1930)

Shermer, Michael, *The Life and Science of Alfred Russel Wallace: A Biographical Study on the Psychology of History* (Oxford: Oxford University Press, 2002)

Steer, Roger, *Dream of Reality* (London: Hodder & Stoughton, 1993)

Stott, John, *Your Mind Matters: The Place of the Mind in the Christian Life* (Leicester: InterVarsity, 1972)

Taylor, John, 'Science, Christianity and the post-modern agenda', *Science and Christian Belief* (October 1998)

Thorpe, W.H., *Purpose in a World of Chance: A Biologist's View* (Oxford: Oxford University Press, 1978)

Trench, Richard Chenevix, *Notes on the Parables of our Lord* (London: Kegan Paul, Trench, 1886)

Van Till, Howard J., 'Basil, Augustine, and the doctrine of creation's functional integrity', *Science and Christian Belief* (April 1996)

Wallace, Alfred R., *Darwinism: An Exposition of the Theory of Natural Selection with Some of its Applications* (London and New York: Macmillan, 1891)

—, *My Life: A Record of Events and Opinions*, 2 vols. (London: Chapman & Hall, 1905)

—, *Man's Place in the Universe* (London: Chapman & Hall, 1908)

—, *The World of Life: A Manifestation of Creative Power, Directional Mind and Ultimate Purpose* (London: Chapman & Hall, 1910)

Ward, Wilfred, 'Tennyson: A Reminiscence' in *Problems and Persons* (London: Longman Green, 1903)

Wells, Jonathan, 'Making sense of biology: the evidence for development by design', *Touchstone* (July/August 1999), 51–55

Wilson, A.N., *God's Funeral* (London: John Murray, 1999)